Dedication

To my mother,
and to her granddaughter, Sandra,
and her husband, Tom Robinson,
without whom this book would never
have happened! They have been so willing and so
able–where could one find their equals?
Theirs should be the credit completely!
Working with them has been a great joy for me, and they
have made my nineties very satisfying years!

Acknowledgements

With much appreciation to Inez Mostue for her gift of the *nisse* which inspired this book's cover, and to Hilma (Lundby) Stadstad for her *rosemaling* designs which grace its pages.

Many thanks to Machelle Sayler who read the folktales, creatively envisioned their depiction, and produced the many delightful illustrations found in *Folkeminnevitskap* and again here in *Folkeminnevitskap II*.

I wish to express my gratitude to Rochelle Wetsch for promoting my books through *Velkommen*, her Scandinavian shop in Grand Forks, ND, and for generously sharing with me her marketing expertise.

I wish to thank the University of Chicago Press for permitting the use of several folktales printed in <u>Folktales of Norway</u> edited by R. Th. Christiansen and translated by Pat Shaw Iversen.

Sincere thanks to Bishop Olav Jakob Tveit for permitting the use of his article, *"Tusser And Trolls In The Mountain At Snarum."*

Thanks to Martin McNamee and the staff of Fine Print of Grand Forks, Inc. for their enthusiasm and expertise.

Foreword

"Preserving our heritage" seems the general theme for the various ethnic groups these days, and the Norwegians are doing much to enhance their own legacy. Childhood memories and family traditions concerning the music, the dress, the foods, and the crafts all serve to enrich our lives and appreciate our heritage.

One more area must be included: the oral tradition, which the storytellers–the *skalds*–preserved from one generation to the next. Eventually these stories were put into a written form: in Iceland through the Eddas–the <u>Poetic Edda</u> and the <u>Prose Edda</u>–by Snorri Sturluson, and in Norway through the *<u>Folke og Huldre Eventyr</u>* by Asbjørnsen and Moe.

The 19th century Sven Grundtvig wrote:

> *Ren og klar,*
> *   skal Nutid føre*
> *Fortids røst*
> *   til Fremtids øre.*

A translation never does justice to the original, but the message is clear:

> Pure and clear,
>   it is the duty of the Present
> to bring the voices of the Past
>   to the ears of the Future.

This is the aim of this writer.

U.S. Copyright pending

ISBN 0-9744422-1-6

Inquiries about this book should be addressed to:
Norwegian Folktales
891 Raindale Court
Grand Forks, ND 58201

Printed and bound in the United States of America
April 2004

Folkeminnevitskap II

Old Tales Retold by Rakel Erickson

Illustrated by Machelle Sayler

Table of Contents

Introduction

These "Old Tales Retold" in no way presume to be more than a sampling of the wealth of legends and folktales which are available. More than four thousand have been written down! But if someone's curiosity is aroused so further reading will result, then the mission of these tales has been accomplished.

To fully appreciate the "Norwegian-ness" of the tales, one must be aware of the geography of the country: the forests, the mountains, the fjords, the rocks, the waterfalls–all play an important part. So does the very location in the far north where days and nights vary so much with the seasons, where shadows are so long and dark, where the valleys are so deep that often the sun shines in only when it is directly overhead.

It was into such a countryside that two young university students wandered. These two–Peter Asbjørnsen and Jørgen Moe–had read the Grimm Brothers tales collected in Germany and found some of the same tales were told–with some variance–in Norway. In their wanderings they began "sitting in" on story telling sessions in homes and in hostels wherever they found storytellers. Asbjørnsen, whose home was in Oslo, wandered through *Nord Marka* (the area around today's Holmenkollen). Jørgen Moe did his collecting in the Ringerike area where his father lived. The two met and shared materials and methods.

The two first published a pamphlet called *Huldre og Folke Eventyr*–no authors names given. It was well received, so they published several pamphlets more. The university then offered them a stipend to continue the work. Both returned to the university. Asbjørnsen became a zoologist but continued his folktale search on holidays. Jørgen Moe studied theology and later became a bishop. He, too, continued collecting as did his son, Moltke Moe, who made it his life's work. Both influenced many others in the clergy to also add to the legends and folktales in the University Collection. Norway today has one of the richest collections and has continued its financial support of scholarly research.

Moe and Asbjørnsen set a style and a standard, which has been carefully followed. Rather than use the dialect of the region of the teller, they used *landsmaal*, the vernacular of the rural area, which could more easily be understood by all. They carefully used the words and the style of the teller and made every effort to preserve the rhythm of the language so the "Norwegian-ness" would come through even in the written form.

Folktales are–of course!–the stories of the **people**…the oral tradition handed down from generation to generation. In some ways they may become changed, but they are easily recognized and are about the **people**–the folk.

The Legends? Well, the function of the legend seems to be to explain anything which seems to need explaining. A legend is told as something that really did happen and was out-of-the-ordinary and, therefore, has been remembered.

Historical legends are presented **as fact**, and **religious legends** are told **as truth**. But since the emphasis is on the out-of-the-ordinary, legends add little to actual history, but they give a picture of folk belief, which is often today known as superstition.

Because Norwegian is a phonetic language, one may say it is a "free-spelling" language, since each person spells a word as it sounds to him. Since dialects differ greatly, so will spelling. Proper names are often spelled in a variety of ways–and in many areas the Icelandic influence is evident by the use of double letters.

Folkeminnevitskap A long word—yes? Really, three words: beginning with the last, it means **knowledge** of the **memories** of our ancient **ancestors**.

Historical Background

The Vikings

In the beginning…

…But where or when **is** the beginning? Is it with the Phoenicians–the seafarers who ventured out on the Mediterranean through the "Pillars of Hercules" (the Straits of Gibraltar) and even went as far as the British Isles in order to get tin? Or does it begin with the historical legend of Joseph of Arimathea who, as a merchant from Jerusalem, came to buy tin and brought with him his nephew (or grandnephew?) Jesus of Nazareth? Places in England still celebrate this legend: Two churches–St. Albans, named for a martyr, and St. Martins in the Field–are still dedicated to the legend, and here the Romans worshiped while England was part of the Roman Empire.

Whatever we choose as a starting point, we come to England and Ireland, which kept both Christianity and learning alive for centuries.

Then came the Vikings!

These seafarers from Norway and Denmark at first were traders. (The Swedish Vikings went South and East.) The Vikings had little to trade except amber from the Baltic and furs from their forest animals. For a time this went well, but when the Vikings saw what others had–the silks, the jewels, the gold, the spices–they became not traders but raiders! They plundered the cities and ravaged the monasteries, carried off what they were able to take and destroyed what they were forced to leave behind. (According to the Anglo-Saxon Chronicle, such raids began in 787 A.D. forewarned by a comet as an omen! The raids continued until about 1000 A.D. The Venerable Bede in his "Ecclesiastical History of the English Nation from the Eighth Century" also records these events.)

The Vikings who returned home after the raids benefited greatly from their raids. They brought back much more than plunder: They brought culture, civilization, and Christianity. And they left behind more than destruction and ravaged cities. Many stayed on, made their homes there, and intermarried. Their children became physically stronger, and their elders taught them their codes of loyalty, law and order. Many descendants became strong leaders, among them Roland and William the Conqueror.

"When we realize all that the Norsemen learned on their raids–from the Irish, the English, the French–and the benefits these raids also brought to these people, then we understand that the Viking Period is an important era in our history–yes, in the history of the world!" From *Norge og Nordens Historie* (in translation) by Jens Raabe, p. 27.

The Missionary Kings

Four kings of Norway are often called the "Missionary Kings" for they were responsible for changing Norway from a pagan nation to a Christian nation. They were:

Harald Haarfagre	872-933
Haakon the Good	935-961
Olav Tryggvesøn	995-1000
Olav Haraldson (St. Olav)	1015-1030

Harald Haarfagre
872-933

Before 872, when Harald "the fair haired" reigned, Norway had many "small" kings. These were large landowners who had managed–usually in battle–to conquer others and annex their land and followers. Harald Haarfagre had in this way acquired much land and many followers.

Harald wished to marry the beautiful and wise Gyda. When she was approached, her reply was this: Only when Harald had unified Norway and was its **only** king would she marry him. Harald, who had the same plan, now made a vow that not until he succeeded in unifying Norway would he cut or comb his hair!

By charisma and diplomacy, but most often by sword, Harald made much progress, but he was also greedy and often cruel. When he taxed the *Odelsbonde*, whose land was a heritage, it seemed a sacrilege, and many fled the country: a loss of many fine people! Harald acquired their lands, but since the elite had gone to the Shetlands or the Orkneys they often came back as marauders.

Years passed–Harald Haarfagre's hair had been cut (Gyda had married someone else) and he died in 933 at age eighty. Harald had done much toward unifying Norway but little toward bringing Christianity to Norway (although he, himself, had been baptized in England.)

Haakon the Good
935-961

Harald Haarfagre had many sons. Haakon was the youngest, and he was literally given to King Adelstein of England to be his foster son. Here he was baptized, educated, and brought up as a Christian in both name and spirit.

When his father, King Harald, died, Haakon returned to Norway where he was immediately accepted as king. He tried his best to encourage the people to give up their old pagan ways and accept Christianity. Although they permitted Haakon to keep his belief in the "White Christ," they preferred to keep their old pagan ways, and when voted on at the *ting* (meeting), Christianity was voted down.

Haakon the Good **was** good for Norway: He enforced the laws for **all**, rich and poor alike; he did away with the *odel* tax; he impressed the people by his example in following the Christian teaching. But it took the forceful personalities of the next two "Missionary Kings" to truly bring Christianity to Norway.

(Haakon the Good was followed by Haakon Jarl, who was called Haakon the Evil One. He was the last heathen king of Norway.)

Olav Tryggvesøn
995-1000

There was a man! A blazing comet across the sky! He was the tallest, the strongest, the most handsome, and the champion at every sport! He ruled Norway for only five years, but he is remembered and celebrated in song, in poetry, and in art. His name has brought fame and glory to Norway. In Norway's history it has been said, "Olav Tryggvesøn is like a shooting star that brightly lights up the world for a brief time, and then is extinguished."

Olav Tryggvesøn was the grandson of Harald Haarfagre. He was baptized in England and crowned king of Norway in Trondheim.

His intention was to convert all of Norway to Christianity–and any who refused to be converted (baptized) were to be "eliminated"–and many were! Their options were: be baptized (converted) and become Christians (in **name** if not in spirit), be exiled

(which meant leaving home, land, and perhaps family), or be killed. They could choose to fight Olav–which had the same result.

Olav Tryggvesøn's fiery enthusiasm for Christianity and his charisma made him successful, especially along the west coast where many had earlier been exposed to the "White Christ."

Olav Tryggvesøn was king for only five years. He had much success–but he also had enemies. In the year 1000 his reign ceased. Again Norway was in turmoil, and again there was regression in the progress of the spread of Christianity.

Olav Haraldson (St. Olav)
1015-1030

Now appeared Olav Haraldson, a grandson of Harald Haarfagre. In less than a half year–it seemed a miracle!–Norway was again a country united under one king. During his entire reign King Olav had two objectives: All people should obey the laws, rich and poor alike; and all people should live as Christians, in private as well as in public.

In order to achieve his aims King Olav encouraged the building of churches, one in each parish, as soon as possible. A great many churches were built, a great many legends were told, and King Olav has gone down in history as a National Saint and the perpetual king of Norway: *Rex Perpetuus Norwegiae.*

These were the "Missionary Kings" who, with much help from priests and missionaries from England and Ireland especially, succeeded in unifying Norway into one kingdom and making Norway a Christian nation in spirit as well as in name.

And the names of these kings–Harald, Haakon, and Olav–continue to be the royal names in Norway today.

Legends

King Olav, The National Saint

Norway is full of folk tradition about King Olav who ruled from 1015-1030 A.D. Not only was King Olav considered the National Saint, but he is also the perpetual king of Norway (*rex perpetuus Norwegiae*). Historical legends concerning his activities are found throughout the country. Some tell how springs burst forth if he was thirsty and how passages opened when he needed them.

In his book, <u>Folktales of Norway</u>, Reidar Th. Christiansen has included many legends about St. Olav. Included here are some of those legends telling about St. Olav building churches.

King Olav, Master Builder Of Trondheim Cathedral

From <u>Folktales of Norway</u> edited by R. Th. Christiansen and translated by Pat Shaw Iversen, p. 7. Legend recorded by A. Faye in the 1830's.

The Cathedral in Trondheim is one of the most magnificent churches in the lands here to the north. It has always been like that–especially the way it was when it had its tall beautiful spire. St. Olav could build the church, all right, but he was not able to put up the spire. He did not rightly know what to do, but in his dilemma he promised the sun as payment to the one who could carry out the work. No one dared take on the work of putting up the spire, until a *troll* came. The *troll* lived in Ladehammeren, a mountain just outside the city. He promised to set up the spire for the payment promised on one condition: that St. Olav was not to call him by name–if he should find out what it was.

It happened one night around midnight that St. Olav sailed past Ladehammeren and came below a place called Kjerringa. Then he heard a child crying, while the mother sang to it to make it go to sleep. To comfort the child she sang, "Tvester is coming soon with the 'heavenly gold.'" The king was happy and hurried back to the church. When he got there, the *troll* was already busy putting the golden knob on the vane of the spire.

Then the king shouted, "Tvester, you're putting the vane too far to the west!"

And when the *troll* heard his name, he plunged down from the spire and was killed.

King Olav, Master Builder Of Seljord Church

From <u>Folktales of Norway</u> edited by R. Th. Christiansen and translated by Pat Shaw Iversen, p. 5. This legend has been collected throughout Norway and in many parts of Sweden, the most famous at the Cathedral at Lund where the lullaby is a well-known nursery rhyme. The fairy tale variant form is popular in England, Germany, and Ireland. Rumpelstiltskin and Tom-Tit-Tot are two of the secret names. This legend from Telemark about the Seljord Church was recorded by Pastor Landstad in the 1840's.

In Bringsaas Mountain, in Seljord, there lived a *troll* who was called Skaane. St. Olav had many churches to build and had to get people to help him wherever he went. He came to an agreement with the *troll* in Bringsaas, that the *troll* was to build the church at Seljord and have it ready by a certain time. If, by that time, the king was not able to guess the *troll's* name, the payment for the building would be the sun and the moon–and King Olav's head.

As might be expected, the work went fast, but the king could in no way find out what the *troll's* name was. Time went by, the church was finished except for the spire and the vane, and they were to be put up the next day. And still the king did not know anything about the *troll's* name.

St. Olav was in great distress and prayed to God for help. Then, in the evening, the *troll* went up towards Bringsaas to find a fine, straight billet out of which to make the spire. Then St. Olav heard someone singing inside the mountain. It was the *troll's* wife singing a lullaby for her baby:

"Bye, bye baby,
Skaane's coming soon,
Bringing St. Olav's head,
And the sun and moon
As playthings for the baby!"

Now St. Olav was saved. On the next day, when the *troll* had raised both spire and vane, he stood there proud of his work and certain of his payment. Then he shouted to the king, "Well, King Olav, which way is the church facing now?"

"East and west, Skaane!" answered the king. But then the *troll* became so angry that he fell down from the church tower and was killed. Since then the church has always been called "St. Olav's Church," and it stands there to this very day.

King Olav And The Gyger

From Folktales of Norway edited by R. Th. Christiansen and translated by Pat Shaw Iversen, p. 4. Collected by A. Faye in Ringerike in the 1840's.

Once, when St. Olav came to Sten Farm in Ringerike, he had plans for building a church at Sten, because it was said his mother had lived there. Now a *gyger*–who lived in a mountain, which is called Gyrihaugen to this very day–didn't like this one bit, and she proposed a wager with the king.

"By the time you have finished your church, I'll have built a stone bridge over the fjord here," the *gyger* said.

The king said he'd like to try, but before the *gyger* was halfway finished with the bridge, she heard bells ringing from St. Olav's church. Then the *gyger* became furious, took all the stones she had gathered for the bridge and threw them, from Gyrihaugen, at the church on the other side of the fjord. But none of the stones hit it. Then the *gyger* became even angrier and wrenched off one of her thighs and threw this at the church. What happened next is a matter of dispute. Some say the *gyger* managed to knock down the tower. Others think she aimed too high. But everyone knows that the thighbone fell down in a murky hole behind the church. This hole is called Gjøger Puddle to this very day, and a bad odor always comes up out of this mud hole.

Up in the mountains, on the same side of the fjord as Gyrihaugen, a steep road goes down into a narrow valley called Krokkeleiva. Once, when St. Olav came along this road, a *gjøger* ran out of the mountain and shrieked at the king:

> "St. Olav, with red beard and all,
>   You ride too near my cellar wall!"

But St. Olav only looked at her and said:

> "Stand there in stock and stone,
>   Until I come this way alone!"

And there she stands to this very day!

The Origin Of The *Huldre*-Folk: The Hidden Children Of Eve

From <u>Folktales of Norway</u> edited by R. Th. Christiansen and translated by Pat Shaw Iversen, p. 91. Collected by Odegaard in Valdres before 1917. Stories about Eve's offspring are told throughout Europe.

The Underworld Creatures? I dare say it was Our Lord who created them, too.

Eve, Adam's wife, lived a long time and had ever so many children. She kept on having children long after the time one usually stopped having them, and at last she was ashamed of having so many.

So it was, once, that Our Lord came by and looked in on Eve, and he asked to see her children. She brought out a whole flock, but left some behind, because she thought it embarrassing to have so many now that she was getting to be so old. Our Lord understood

"Where Are the rest?"

this all right, and was a little hurt, and said to Eve: "If you are hiding children from me, then they shall be hidden from you."

Then Eve could not see these children any longer. They were turned into the underworld people: the *haug*-folk, the *trolls*, the *huldre*-folk, the *nisse*, and many others. There is probably not much difference between them and us, because the same one has created them. But they are not Christians like we are.

The Origin Of The *Huldre*-Folk: Lucifer

Another legend about the origin of the huldre-folk developed when listeners heard the story of Lucifer's expulsion from heaven.

The story in Isaiah about the expulsion of Lucifer and his followers from heaven seemed to the Norsemen a very logical explanation of these "Other World" people. As they fell from heaven, some fell in the ocean (the *draug*), some fell in ponds (*nøkken*), many in the mountains (*trolls*), many more on farms (*tusse, nisse, tunkall,* etc.) and many others.

Isaiah Chapter 14:12-15: (King James Version)

How art thou fallen from heaven, O Lucifer, son of the morning! How art thou cut down to the ground, which didst weaken the nations! For thou hast said in thine heart, I will ascend into heaven, I will exalt my throne above the stars of God: I will sit also upon the mount of the congregation, in the sides of the north: I will ascend above the heights of the clouds; I will be like the most High. Yet thou shalt be brought down to hell, to the sides of the pit.

The Origin Of The *Huldre*-Folk:
The *Huldre* Minister

From <u>Folktales of Norway</u> edited by R. Th. Christiansen and translated by Pat Shaw Iversen, p. 89. This folktale was collected in Setesdal by J. Skar (no date). Various legends are found about the reactions of the "Huldre-folk" (or "underworld people") to Christianity.

There was once a farm in the area of Setesdal where the country people had quite a lot of dealing with the *huldre*-folk. One *tusse* was in the habit of coming there and borrowing one thing and another from the farmer. The parson heard tell of this, so one day he took it upon himself to journey to this farm to ask if there was any truth in what people were saying.

"Yes," said the farmer. "If you will sit down for about an hour, you will see the *tusse*. He has borrowed a pot of ale, and the next time the clock strikes, he is returning it."

The parson sat down and waited. When the clock struck, the *tusse* came, put the pot of ale on the table, bowed to the farmer, and turned to leave. But the parson got to the door first and blocked the way, and then he started talking to the *tusse*. The parson preached a sermon from the New Testament. He spoke of "the little babe," and he held forth as though he wanted to convert the *tusse*, for he probably thought the *tusse* was the devil.

The *tusse* said not a word. He struggled and wanted to go out, but the parson held onto the latch and quoted and talked from the scriptures, from one to the other.

The *tusse* never answered a word, but at last he said, "I'm not so learned that I can talk with you, but if you will sit down and wait a bit, I'll fetch my brother. He's a minister just like you." The *tusse* promised that his brother really would come, but the parson dared not let him go, for he was afraid the *tusse* would get away from them.

"You can safely let him go," said the farmer. "If he has promised his brother will come, then he'll come all right. The *tusse* never lies."

So the parson sat down and waited, and after he had been waiting a whole hour, the *tusse* minister came, in frock coat with a ruffled collar, and with a Bible in his hand.

"Do you know the book of Genesis?" asked the *tusse* minister.

Yes, that he did, answered the parson.

"It says there that, in the beginning, God created man and woman. Do you know that?" asked the *tusse* minister.

Yes, the parson knew that, too.

And then the *tusse* minister showed him what it said in the scriptures. "But when the world had been created according to the second chapter, God then made a woman out of Adam's rib. Do you know that?" asked the *tusse* minister.

Yes, that the parson knew.

"Then Adam said: '**This time**'–why did he say '**this time**'? Do you know that?" asked the *tusse* minister.

No, the parson did not know that.

Then the *tusse* minister said, "That woman, who was created in the very beginning, was Adam's equal in every way, and would never be under him in anything. She considered herself just as good a creation as Adam. But God said it wasn't good for man and woman to be equal, so God sent her and her children away, and put them into the hills to live. They are without sin, and they stay there inside the hills, except when they themselves want to be seen," the *tusse* minister continued. "But in the second chapter, God took a rib out of Adam's side and made a woman out of it, and then Adam said, '**This time**' because she was

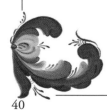

taken out of the man. Her offspring have sin, and that is why God had to give them the New Testament. The *tusse*-folk only need the Old."

The parson had to give in to the *tusse* minister in everything, and he never went back in the pulpit again. The name of Adam's first wife is never mentioned in the Bible. She's called Lilli–or was it Lillo? But there's not much difference.

Tusser And *Trolls* In The Mountain At Snarum

In 1983 this article appeared in the church paper in the Heggen Parish in Modum. Later, research on family history from the area "uncovered" the same incident. A strange coincidence! The article–in translation–is included here in its entirety with the kind consent of Bishop Olav Jakob Tveit. Our sincere thanks to him!

In Snarum one can hear several "true" legends about people who were lured by *trolls* into the Knoll down by the Snarum River. Whenever this happened–so the legend goes–people would ring the church bells. Then the *trolls* would lose their magic power and their captives would be freed. But sometimes it happened that the *trolls* became so irritated by all the bell ringing that they would throw stones at the church. To this day stones can be seen beside the church to prove the legend is true.

Legends such as this are found in many places, but this one at Snarum is very well documented. The legend here has a famous sequel: In 1687 there was an important court case with lengthy sessions and more than thirty witnesses, several of whom were sentenced for having rung the church bells at an improper time, and for having misused the name of God in order to recover a child supposedly taken into the mountain by a *troll*.

From where I sit here in my parsonage at Snarum I can look right down to the mountain called The Knoll at Snarum. It is dark, weird, mysterious-looking and drops steeply toward the water. If there are gnomes and *trolls*, this Knoll would make an excellent home for them.

It is strange to sit here and think about those who lived in this community before us. What kind of people were they? What did they do? One thing is certain: they were much troubled by a fear of the unknown–of the supernatural, the underworld, and the evil spirits. Just imagine having to walk by that dark Knoll in the evening–or in the dark of night!–and feel you might be taken into the mountain by a *troll*!

There are many legends about those taken by force into the mountain. The stories are that now and then the *trolls* would steal a young beautiful girl, and she would become a *troll's* wife. Later, when a child was expected, the *troll* would steal a midwife from the community. Sometimes people were "set free" and returned to their homes–but rarely. Most disappeared into the mountain forever. Legend has it that a few managed to escape while the church bells were ringing. They ran home as quickly as they could! One poor soul had her hand on the door handle at home when the bell rope in the tower broke–and she was again under the *troll's* magic spell, so back to the mountain she went. People sometimes met their "stolen" people wandering in the forest on the Knoll. Some were probably married to *trolls*, so were forever under the *troll's* spell. All they could do was send one last greeting to their parents at home.

The most famous–or infamous!–*troll* in the Knoll was called Trond With The Tooth because he had an ugly fang-like tooth which reached far down on his chin. He constantly prowled around the community trying to exchange ugly *troll* babies with the babies of ordinary humans. Even on Christmas Eve he would slyly sneak around the homes. All were on the lookout for him. Yes, this was the biggest problem with the underworld characters at Snarum, whether *tusser* or *trolls*, that they were so eager to exchange children.

The Changeling at Lofthus

Right by the church at Snarum is a farm called Lofthus. A child was born there who was not quite "right." All those who knew about such things were sure of what had happened: The mountain people in the Knoll had been up to their tricks again! They had left a *troll* child in the cradle to replace the Lofthus child! So—now there was a "changeling" at Lofthus.

But a beggar-woman said she knew what should be done: On a Thursday night the mother was to take the changeling to the mountain; then, while others rang the church bells, she was to cry, "Change back! Change back!" So plans were made. Many well-known farmers from Snarum would come along and help with the bell ringing; others were on the Knoll.

On the third Thursday Saddle Maker Anders Olsen from East Modum was

The mother stood holding her child there at the base of the mountain by the Snarum River and called, "Byt om! Byt om!" ("Exchange! Exchange!") while the church bells were ringing.

- Illustrated by: Anne Signe Høyroll

brought in. He was known as one who could cast a spell over–or exorcise–the evil spirits. This was on All Saints Day in 1683.

The saddle maker cut branches from a birch tree. Using these, he whipped the mountain, calling loudly: "If there is a door, and if someone is inside, then–Open! And come out in the Name of the Father, and the Son, and the Holy Ghost!" At the same time, more was happening: The mother and child–and many others with her!–stood at the foot of the mountain crying, "Change back! Change back!" And all the while the church bells were ringing!

But in spite of the whipping and ringing and calling, the mountain people were not persuaded to return the child, so people went home disappointed this evening, also.

The Court Case

But this incident had a sequel: Some of the people in the community who knew of the happening but had not been involved, complained to the officials about this in 1683. The result was that in 1687 a number of people from the area were called in to the Maelum Court Room at Aamot and charged with blasphemy. The legal case became an extended one with lengthy discussions and more than thirty witnesses. Ringing the church bells off schedule was punishable by law, and for the practice of black magic and witchcraft one could lose both property and life. Old heathen superstitions must be eradicated!

The Judgment

Sentences were pronounced May 2, 1687. The parents, the saddle maker, and all those who had been with the mother and child at the Knoll were judged to have blasphemed. They were ordered to make confession in church and also pay a fine to the Oslo hospital.

Those who had only rung the church bells escaped with mere confession. Others, who had participated either in fun or innocence, mostly young people, were acquitted but were admonished "never to be prevailed upon to participate in such sinful doings again."

Well, this judgment is an interesting testimonial from the distant past in a little community in our parish. It shows people's thinking and their desperation when something was the matter with their children. It also shows the serious determination of the authorities to overcome superstition. The sentences imposed were, we must say, mild since they were given during those otherwise cruel times.

Disposing Of A Changeling:
The Changeling In The Field

From <u>Folktales of Norway</u> edited by R. Th. Christiansen and translated by Pat Shaw Iversen, p. 93. Collected by Ivar Aasen in Western Norway in 1884.

There was once a farmer who needed his wife's help in the field. She had a tiny baby, but like other mothers, she put her baby in a little cradle, which she carried to the field with her.

It so happened that she had to leave the cradle for a while as the baby slept. When she came back, **her** child was gone, and in its place was another baby–tiny, hungry, and dirty.

The mother called to her husband who came running. At once the husband took the child out into the field where he put it down. Then he shouted toward the woods that whoever placed the child there must come at once and take it back and leave **his** child instead. If they did not do so, he would shout and scream and crash about in the woods until the ground shook, and they would never be left in peace until they did as he said.

Then the husband left the child in the field and went back to his work. But as he went, he turned and looked back. He saw a *hulder* come and exchange the children and slip back into the woods with her own child as fast as she could. Both the farmer and his wife were very happy, for their own child was with them again.

And how did the husband know a *hulder* had made the exchange?–As she leaned over to make the exchange, he saw the cow's tail below her skirt!

Disposing Of A Changeling:
The *Nisse* Changeling

Collected in Telemark. A tale widely told, especially in Eastern Norway.

A *nisse* is usually satisfied with his occasional bowl of porridge, especially if it has a good-sized "butter-eye." But in Telemark there once lived a *nisse* who **may** have been a changeling! No one could remember when he was born or when he came to the farm. No one had ever heard him speak; yet all were afraid to do anything to make him angry. He ate so much that the people at this farm had lived in poverty for generations.

One day a wise woman came and told them what to do. They were to take their biggest pot and in it cook only as much porridge as needed for a tiny baby. This pot was to be put in the middle of the floor, around it they were to put their largest bowls, and in the bowls they were to put as many big spoons as they could find. When this was done, they were all to go out so the *nisse* changeling was alone in the house.

The people watched–unseen–as the *nisse* changeling walked around and peered into the pot and bowls. Then they heard him speak for the first, and last, time: "Never before have I seen such a **big** pot, so **many** bowls, such **huge** spoons, and so **little** food!"

Then the *nisse* left, never to be seen again.

The *Tunkall*

From <u>Folktales of Norway</u> edited by R. Th. Christiansen and translated by Pat Shaw Iversen, p. 141. Traditions about the tunkall as guardian of the house belong in northern and western Norway. Traditions about nisse come from the east and south.

On Steintland Farm, in Hjelmeland, there was a *tunkall* in the old days. Many people lived on the farm, but all of the houses stood close together as that was a custom on big farms at that time. A little apart from the houses was the sheep shed, and it was there the *tunkall* usually stayed. Whenever people went by this sheep shed in the evening, they could hear the *tunkall* grunting like a pig.

There also was an old shack on the farm, and in it was a bed that always stood ready for the *tunkall*. Otherwise no one else lived in this shack. If there was no bedding or straw, they could hear the *tunkall* wailing and carrying on. In the morning it always looked as if a dog had slept there.

An old woman on the farm said that she could both hear and see the *tunkall*. Yes, she often talked with him, for they were really good friends. When the old woman became sick, they heard the *tunkall* crying and wailing, and when the old woman died, the *tunkall* disappeared, and no one has ever seen him since.

The *Gardvord* Beats Up The *Troll*

From <u>Folktales of Norway</u> edited by R. Th. Christiansen and translated by Pat Shaw Iversen, p. 143.
This was collected by Ivar Aasen in Sogn (western Norway) in 1842. The gardvord is another name for
the tunkall.

A hunter–his name was Tore Nabben–was up in the mountains hunting. When night
came, he went to sleep in a bunk in a *seter*. In the middle of the night he heard
shouting from the hill:

> "Will you lend me that big cauldron?
> I want to cook ol' Tore Nabben!"

Then came the reply:

> "Yes, if I can taste the broth!"

Soon came the answer:

> "Before the broth you can try,
> on the coals he will fry!"

Tore became frightened, and he hurried off as fast as he could. When he had come a
little bit on the way he met a *gardvord* with a pole on his back. Tore hurried even faster,
and when he had come a bit farther on the way, he heard a terrible shrieking behind

him. He dared not look back, but ran and ran until he reached home.

The next day Tore took his brother along, and they went back to the same place where Tore had been during the night. There they saw blood and other signs that the *gardvord* had beaten the *troll* to death.

Outrunning A *Hulder*

From Folktales of Norway *edited by R. Th. Christiansen and translated by Pat Shaw Iversen, p. 128. This story was collected by a schoolteacher, Fosse, in Sogn in about 1935.*

A grown young man from Systrand spent a winter snaring grouse up at a *seter* in the parish. The young man had his dog with him.

One evening, as the young man was sitting by the hearth cooking his food, he heard something rattling outside against the wall. It sounded as if someone were leaning something against the wall. The *seter* was made of stone and had a turf roof. Shortly after, someone came in the entryway and knocked at the door. The dog barked and its hair stood on end, and then in came a beautiful maiden. The boy had never seen so beautiful a maiden before. She was wearing a red bodice and a blue skirt, and she had long, fair hair, which hung down her back. The boy was quite amazed that a girl would come to the *seter* in the middle of the winter. It was seven miles to town, and the snow was deep.

The girl started talking to the young man and asked if he did not think it was lonely to stay up in the *seter* in the middle of the winter. She laughed and talked, turning and twisting, and showing off to him. The young man answered back, laughing and joking, and thought this was really fine. At last he asked if she would stay there. Then it would not be so lonely any more. A strange expression came over the girl's face, and she turned away from him, and then the young man saw that she had a long tail which hung below her skirt. Now he understood that the girl was a *hulder* and that she

wanted to marry him. He had heard that *huldre*-folk liked to marry Christians. The young man became afraid of her and thought he had better watch his step here, for he was halfway engaged to a girl down in the parish. When the girl turned around, he did not join in the joking any longer. The girl went on talking and laughing as before and asked if he did not like girls. But he did not say much to that.

After a time, the young man found some pretext for going outside, and the dog went with him. The moon was full and shining brightly. Then he caught sight of the *hulder's* skis, which she had leaned up against the wall of the *seter*. They were made of brass and gleamed and shone in the moonlight. He put them on, took her poles, and set out down the mountain toward the parish. The skis slid over the snow unusually fast, and the young man went at such a speed that the dog could not keep up with him.

When the young man did not come back in again, the *hulder* grew suspicious and went outside to look. She soon caught sight of him heading down the mountain at a good clip. When she looked for her skis, she found the young man had taken them. Then the *hulder* became furious because he had wanted to run away from her. She put on his skis and took his poles and set out after him. But they were only poor fir skis with willow bindings, so they went much slower than her own. She did not catch up with the young man, but she did catch up with the dog and broke its back with the ski pole.

But the young man got home, and the brass skis are still supposed to be at Henja Farm to this very day.

Married To A *Hulder*

From <u>Folktales of Norway</u> edited by R. Th. Christiansen and translated by Pat Shaw Iversen, p. 110. This legend was collected by Kjell Flatin in Telemark in 1912 or 1913. (First printed in 1930.) This legend was known in southern and central Norway, and there are about 150 variants—only seven from the north.

One summer Olav Lonar was fishing up in the mountains far to the north. There were plenty of fish, but there was no denying that others fished there after dark. Olav usually remained up there for long periods of time to chase away the thieves. He stayed in an old *seter*.

One evening as Olav was about to go to bed, he had an errand outside. He went out the door, but before he knew where he was, he found himself standing inside a big, richly furnished room. A fire was burning on the hearth, and on the walls gleamed silver goblets, pewter plates, and copper kettles. Over by the hearth sat an old man and an old woman. A beautiful young maiden went back and forth. She put food and drink of the very best sort on the table and invited Olav to sit down. But Olav understood that something was wrong, and he dared not eat or drink.

"You needn't be afraid to eat or drink here," said the old fellow over by the hearth. "We won't do you any harm. You shall leave here as freely as you came."

The maiden was quite sweet tempered. She stole a glance at Olav every now and then. Olav thought he had never seen such a beautiful girl before, but he sat there like a block of wood and was not able to utter a word, nor would he eat or drink anything either.

All at once–and he did not understand how it had happened–Olav was standing outside the door of his *seter* again. Everything was dark and cold, and there was barely a faint glow in the coals over in the hearth. For his part, Olav thought he had only been outside for a little while. But when he went to look, the big birch logs had burned up and only a few coals were left. Olav had put the logs on the fire for the night before he went out, and now he understood that it must have been some time ago. Olav went to bed and had a quiet, restful sleep.

But the maiden Olav had seen that evening was never out of his thoughts, no matter where he went. He tried to get her out of his mind, but it was no use. All that autumn and winter Olav went about like a half-wit and was changed beyond recognition. He did not open his mouth and appeared not to see or hear.

The next summer Olav was up in the mountains again, keeping an eye on the fish. Then one evening he went outside the door. Before he knew it, Olav found himself in the same room with the old couple and the young maiden he had met the previous summer. Everything happened as before. The maiden went back and forth and was so fine and beautiful that she was a joy to behold. She put the very best food and drink on the table, and now Olav was not careful any longer. He sat down at the table and helped himself. Now the old couple started to speak, and said that they had thought of giving their daughter, the beautiful maiden, to Olav. And they promised that good fortune and prosperity would follow him and his family all their days. Olav thought he had never heard anything better, and so they were engaged–he and the *tusse* maiden. Her name was Torgun.

Olav stayed up in the mountains a long time that summer, and the people back home almost gave up waiting for him. But late in the autumn, when he came down, Torgun was with him. Folks in the parish were not a little surprised that Olav Lonar had found a wife. No one knew where she was from or whether she had any kinfolk. Then the wedding was held, and Olav was married to Torgun in the church. At the wedding people noticed that Torgun had a long tail, and then they understood who she was. But when Torgun went in through the church door, the tail fell off, and Olav never saw anything of it again.

They all thought Torgun was the prettiest and finest looking woman they had ever seen. She was quiet-spoken and did not put on airs; she was careful not to do anything wrong and was kind to rich and poor alike. Poor folk who came to the farm begging for food were never turned away; they never left without having something to take with them. Torgun was known for her kindness, and poor folk came from far and wide. Everything prospered after Torgun came there. The cows gave more milk and were so fat and sleek that no one had ever seen anything like it.

The first winter they were at Lonar, Torgun and Olav had a falling-out about what to do with the newborn calves. Olav wanted to follow the old custom of breeding the prettiest calves, but Torgun insisted that they be butchered.

"What are you thinking of, woman? Do you want to take the lives of the ones that will make the best cows?" said Olav.

"Don't worry about that," said Torgun.

In the spring, when they let out the animals, Olav was not a little surprised, for every one of the cows had a fine calf with her.

"How in all the world can this be," said Olav, "when we've butchered all the calves?"

"Every cow had two calves, but my mother won't take any away from us!" said Torgun. The calves grew and thrived, and became big, splendid-looking cows, and no one had ever seen anything like the herd they had at Lonar.

Olav was not nice to his wife. He was quarrelsome and ill-tempered and scolded her from morning till night. Torgun kept quiet and never made a fuss about it. But one Sunday Olav and Torgun were going to church. Olav was out in the yard struggling with the horse. He wanted to put on a horseshoe, but he could not get it to fit the way it should. Olav cursed and swore and carried on as if he were out of his mind. Torgun could not stand hearing anyone swear, and now she went out to Olav and stood staring at him for a while. Then she took the horseshoe and wadded it up with her bare hands. Then she straightened it out again, fitted it to the hoof, and bent it a little more at the ends.

"This is the way a horseshoe should fit," Torgun said, and looked sharply at Olav.

"You're more than a woman, Torgun," said Olav. "As bad as I've been to you more than once, and you haven't hauled off and given me a thrashing! I think that's strange!"

"I've got better sense," said Torgun.

After this, Olav was a different person. He never swore so Torgun could hear it, and he was accommodating and kind to her in every way. Torgun and Olav became very rich. They had good luck with everything they did, and there was such prosperity and everything grew so well at the farm that it was downright strange to see. Their descendants were also rich, and have lived in Lonar parish until now, and Torgun's name has remained in the family.

The New Breeches

From Folktales of Norway edited by R. Th. Christiansen and translated by Pat Shaw Iversen, p. 138. Collected by Kr. Bugge in eastern Norway about 1905. Twelve Norwegian variants have been found.

On a farm in Jarlsberg–as far as I know–they had a *nisse* who was kind and helpful. But he could get angry, too, and then the *nisse* was not easy to get along with. When the *nisse* was angry he would do things like putting the new-born calves down in the bucket or pouring out the milk for the dairymaid and many other tricks. So both the farmer and the dairymaid thought it best to satisfy the *nisse* in everything within reason, and they certainly did not regret it either. The dairymaid took care to put out really fine cream porridge in the barn every holiday, and on Christmas Eve she put an extra big lump of butter in it so the porridge would be rich and good.

It was easy to see that the *nisse* appreciated all the good things he got, for nowhere did the cows thrive as well as on that farm. Not to mention the horses! For the *nisse* had given most of his love and care to them. When the farmer came home, he didn't even have to put the horses in. The farmer just unharnessed them, and the *nisse* took care of the rest. The *nisse* put the horses in the stable, rubbed them down with a handful of straw, took down hay to them, and gave them water. The farmer knew this, so he let the *nisse* take care of the horses the way the *nisse* liked. And, as the farmer was so well satisfied with the *nisse* in every way, he put a fine pair of white leather breeches out for the *nisse* one day.

One day the farmer and his son were out driving. When they got home it was raining

as though the heavens had opened, so they left the horses standing outside and hurried into the house. They thought the *nisse* would put the horses in the stable the way he usually did. But the one who didn't come, that was the *nisse*. The farmer and his son went to the window to see how the horses were getting along, and there stood the *nisse*, quite content, in the door of the stable, with his hands deep in the pockets of his new leather breeches.

The farmer was annoyed, as you can imagine, so he went to the door and shouted, "My good *nisse*, what does this mean? Don't you **see** the horses today?"

The *nisse* slapped his thighs with both hands and laughed so hard he almost fell over. Then he straightened up, stuck out one leg, thrust his hands down in his pockets again, and said, "Well, you certainly don't expect me to go out in this weather with my new white leather breeches on, do you?"

The *Nisse's* Revenge

From <u>Folktales of Norway</u> edited by R. Th. Christiansen and translated by Pat Shaw Iversen, p. 140. There are about forty variants of this story, which P. C. Asbjørnsen localized in Hallingdal—but he first collected it in Christiania (Oslo) in 1845.

There was once a girl at a farm—I believe it was in Hallingdal—who was going to take a bowl of *rømmegrøt*, cream porridge, out to the *nisse*. Now this was either on a Thursday evening or on Christmas Eve—I don't remember—but this was most likely on Christmas Eve, because shouldn't the *nisse* have an especially good feast so he would bring the farm good luck during the coming year? And this was a large bowl of warm *rømmegrøt* with a generous "*smør-øye*," butter-eye, melting in it.

Now the girl thought it was a pity to give this good food to the *nisse*, so she ate the *rømmegrøt* while it was still warm and drank all the melted butter from the butter-eye, too. And what did she bring the *nisse*? Some cold oatmeal porridge with sour milk on it in a pig's trough!

"Here is your trough, you nasty old thing!" she said. But before she had finished saying this, the *nisse* rushed in and grabbed her and began to dance. The *nisse* kept it up, dancing **wildly**, and as he danced, he sang:

> "Oh, the *nisse's* porridge you did steal!
> So dance with the *nisse* until you reel!"

The *nisse* kept dancing and singing until the girl lay on the ground gasping for breath, and when people came to the barn the next morning, the girl was more dead than alive.

The *Nisse* Moves

One Norwegian farmer who was tired of his *nisse's* tricks decided to move away from him. So the farmer loaded his belongings into a wagon and tied the cow behind. He started down the road to his new home. Just as they passed a neighbor's farm, a trunk on the top of the load flew open, and the *nisse* stuck his head out.

"We're moving today!" the *nisse* shouted gleefully.

An Old Norwegian song:
"*Gammel Stev*" melody.

Og mannen ville fra nissen flytte.
Men reisen blev ham til liten nytte.
Ti høit fra vogn lasset nissen lo,
"Jeg tror vi flytte idag, vi to!"

Translation:

The farmer wanted to move away.
Without the man *nisse* wouldn't stay.
The trunk popped open along the way,
And laughing, *nisse* said, "We move today!"

Folktales

The Cat On Dovre Mountain

From <u>Folktales of Norway</u> *edited by R. Th. Christiansen and translated by Pat Shaw Iversen, p. 121. This story is well known throughout Norway. It was collected by P. Chr. Asbjørnsen in Gudbrandsdal in 1852. Over 200 variants have been collected! (One literary critic said this was the best cat story ever written—and there is not a cat in it!)*

There was once a man up in Finnmark who had caught a big white bear which he was going to take to the king of Denmark. While on his way it so happened that he was near Dovre Mountain on Christmas Eve, and there he went into a cottage where lived a man whose name was Halvor. The man asked Halvor if he could get a room for himself and his bear for the night.

"Heaven help me if what I say is not true," said Halvor, "but we can't give anyone a room just now, for every Christmas Eve such a pack of *trolls* come down on us that we are forced to flee and haven't as much as a roof over our own heads, to say nothing of lending one to anyone else!"

"Oh," said the man, "if that is all, you can very well lend me your house. My bear can lie under the stove, and I can sleep in the closet."

Well, the man begged so hard that at last he got Halvor's permission to stay there, and the people of the house moved out. But before they left, everything was made ready for the *trolls*. The tables were set, the rice porridge was ready, the fish was boiled, the sausages were hot, and everything else that was good–just as for any other grand feast.

So, when everything was ready, down came the *trolls* from Dovre. Some were large and some were small, some had long tails and some had no tails at all, some, too, had long, long noses. The *trolls* ate and they ate, and they drank and they drank, and they tasted everything.

Suddenly one of the little *trolls* caught sight of the white bear, which lay under the stove. So the little *troll* took a piece of sausage, stuck it on a stick, and went and poked it at the bear's nose, screaming out, "Pussy, will you have some sausage?"

Then the white bear rose up, growling fiercely, and chased the whole pack of *trolls* out of the door, both great and small.

The next Christmas Halvor was out in the woods in the afternoon of Christmas Eve cutting wood for the holidays, for he thought the *trolls* would come again. Just as he was hard at work, he heard a voice in the woods calling out, "Halvor! Halvor!"

"Well," said Halvor, "here I am!"

"Have you got your big cat with you still?" asked the *troll*.

"Yes, that I have!" said Halvor. "She's lying at home under the stove. And what's more, she now has seven kittens far bigger and fiercer than she is herself!"

"Oh! Then we will never come to see you again!" called out the *troll* from far away in the woods. And he has kept his word, for since that time the *trolls* have never eaten their Christmas dinner with Halvor on Dovre Mountain.

Halvor!
Halvor!

The *Trolls* Of Hedal Forest

Man could overcome the forces of evil and darkness by his own wit and humor.

On a place called Vaage in Gudbrandsdal there once, in olden days, lived a very poor couple who had many children. Two of the sons who were half-grown, one a bit older than the other, spent much of the time wandering around in the neighborhood begging. Since they were constantly roaming, they knew all the roads and paths as well as the shortcut through the marsh to Hedal.

One day the two boys decided to go to Hedal. They had heard that some bird catchers had built a cabin along the way. The boys wanted to see how the men captured the falcons, so they took the shortcut, which would take them near the falconer's hut. It was late in the fall, the *seters* were deserted, and there was no place for them to get food or shelter. They tried to stay on the path to Hedal, but this was a small, narrow path, seldom used and hard to see. When darkness fell they lost the path and did not find the bird catchers' cabin. Before they knew it, they were deep in the thick Bjølstad woods, a part of the large Hedal Forest. The boys realized they could not find their way in the darkness, so they started a fire, cut branches for some shelter, and gathered heather for a bed. Then they lay down to sleep.

When they were almost asleep, they heard something sniffing and snuffling as if smelling its way. The boys put their ears to the ground to hear if any animal was near–or even a forest *troll!* Then the "something" sniffed and snuffled **loudly** and a voice said, "I smell Christian Blood!"

And then the boys heard a step so heavy that the earth shook–and they **knew** the *trolls* were out!

"Oh–God help us! What shall we do now?" asked the younger brother.

"You stand–and keep standing!–under this evergreen, but be ready to grab your begging bag and run. I'll take the little axe," said the older boy.

Just then they saw the *trolls*!–three *trolls* so enormous their heads were even with the tops of the trees! And the three *trolls* had only one eye, which they shared. This they took turns using. Each had a hollow in his forehead in which he placed the eye and used his hand to direct it. The *troll* who led the way carried the eye. The others followed, holding on to the first *troll*.

"Now–move!" said the older brother, "but don't go too far before you see what happens. Since the eye is up so high it will be hard for them to see me if I come behind them–or under them!"

So the younger brother ran ahead, and the *trolls* followed. Meanwhile, the older brother followed with his little axe, watched his chance and then struck the ankle of the last *troll*, who shrieked so loudly he startled the first *troll*–who dropped the eye! The boy was **not** slow to pick it up! The eye was as large as two saucers placed together, and when the boy looked into it, he could see as clearly as if in daylight–yet it was as dark as midnight.

When the *trolls* understood the boy had taken the eye and had injured one *troll's* foot,

they began making horrible threats telling what they would do if the boy did not **at once** return the eye to them.

"I'm not afraid of *trolls* and their threats," said the boy, "for now I have **three** eyes and you don't have any! Besides, two of you must carry the third if you are to go anywhere!"

"If you don't give us our eye again **now, at once**, you shall turn into sticks and stones!" threatened the *trolls*.

But the boy thought there was no rush now that there was no danger. He wasn't afraid of either their bragging or their *troll* magic. Besides, he told them, maybe he ought to give each one a cut with his axe so they could all crawl around on the ground like worms or snakes.

When the *trolls* heard this, they became afraid and changed their tune. They now said if the boy would return their eye, they would give him gold and silver—and more!

Yes, the boy thought that would be good, but he wanted the gold and silver before he gave up the eye! If one *troll* would go home and bring back two steel bows and enough treasure to fill his brother's bag, then he would give up the eye.

The *trolls* complained loudly that no one could find his way home without the eye, but just then one *troll* began shrieking for their wife—for they had one wife for the three of them! They all shouted and called so their voices echoed and re-echoed in the mountains. Finally they heard an answer from far away. It was the wife. The *trolls*

told her to come with two steel bows and two pails of gold and silver.

Before long the wife was there. When she heard their tales, she, too, began threatening them with *troll* craft and witches' spells, but the *trolls* begged her not to threaten the boys and to beware of "the little wasp" as they called the one with the axe. He might take her eye, too! Finally she agreed.

She threw down the two bows, poured the gold and silver into the brother's bag, and hurried away with the three *trolls* and their one eye.

And since that time no one has ever heard that the *trolls* have again gone walking in the Hedal Forest looking for Christian Blood!

Askeladden's Eating Contest With The *Troll*

The normal values of truth and helpfulness did not apply when dealing with "forces of darkness" such as trolls. Here wit and humor were needed!

There was once a peasant who had three sons—Peter, Paul, and Espen *Askeladden*. The peasant was old and weak and unable to keep up with the work. He had hoped his son would cut down the trees in the woods, sell them, and earn enough to pay his debt. But—the sons were lazy.

Finally the peasant convinced his eldest son, Peter, to take his axe and go to the woods to begin the work. When at last Peter reached the woods and began to chop down a tree, a huge *troll* appeared.

"If you chop down my forest, I'm going to kill you!" said the *troll*.

When Peter heard this, he threw down his axe and ran home as fast as he could. All out of breath he told his father what had happened.

"Peter! You have the heart of a rabbit to be so easily frightened! The *trolls* never frightened me when I was young!" exclaimed his father.

The next day Paul started off for the woods. Exactly the same thing happened. Paul had made just a few cuts with his axe when the *troll* appeared and shouted, "If you chop down trees in my woods, I'm going to kill you!"

Paul scarcely dared look at the *troll*. He did just as his brother had done. He threw down his axe and ran home as fast as his legs could carry him!

The father was again angry and told Paul the *trolls* had never frightened him when he was young.

The third day Espen *Askeladden* wanted to go.

"Oh, you! You!" said the two older brothers. "You think you will finish the job!—You who have scarcely been outside the door!"

Askeladden didn't even answer his brothers, but he asked for some food to take with him. His mother had no cheese, so she curdled some milk and sent the curds with him in his knapsack, and away he went. He had walked just a short way when the *troll* rushed at him and screamed, "If you cut down my trees, I will kill you!"

But *Askeladden* was not slow. He ran to his knapsack, took out the curds and squeezed and squeezed them so the whey splattered. Then he told the *troll*, "If you don't keep still, I shall squeeze you as hard as I am squeezing water from this white stone!"

"Oh, no! Please spare my life!" begged the *troll*. "I'll help you cut down trees!"

Askeladden promised that if the *troll* would help cut down the trees, he—*Askeladden*—would spare the *troll's* life.

The *troll* was a good worker, and many trees were cut down before evening. Then the *troll* said, "Now you can come home with me because my house is much nearer than yours." *Askeladden* went with him.

When they arrived, the *troll* said he would build the fire while the boy went to get water for the porridge pot.

There stood the two big pails, so big and heavy the boy could not even move them. So he called to the *troll*, "It isn't worth the bother to take these two thimbles. I'll just bring the entire well to the house!"

"Oh, no! I must keep my well!" said the *troll*. "Why don't **you** build the fire, and **I** will go get the water."

When the *troll* came back with the water, they boiled up a big pot full of porridge.

"If it's all the same with you," said Espen *Askeladden*, "let's have a race to see who can eat the most."

"Oh, yes!" said the *troll*, sure that he could win this race.

So they sat down at the table–but the boy, unnoticed, took his leather knapsack, opened it and tied it in front of him–and as he ate, he put more into his knapsack than into his stomach.

When the knapsack was filled, the boy took out his knife and slit the knapsack open. The *troll* looked at him, but said nothing. When they had eaten a good while longer, the *troll* put his spoon down.

"No–now I can't eat any more!" said the *troll*.

"Oh, you must eat," said the boy. "I'm only half through! Do as I do–cut a slit in your stomach–then you can eat as much as you like!"

"But doesn't it hurt?" asked the *troll*.

"Oh–nothing worth mentioning," said *Askeladden*.

So the *troll* did what the boy said–and that was the end of the *troll*.

But Espen *Askeladden* looked around at all the silver and gold found in the *troll's* mountain home, and he went home with enough to pay off his father's debt.

The Boy And The Devil

There was once a boy who walked along the way shelling some hazelnuts. Among the nuts the boy found one with a wormhole in it–and just then he met the devil.

"Is it true what they say," asked the boy, "that the devil can make himself as small as he wants to and can even force himself through a pin hole?"

"Oh, yes, that I can do!" answered the devil.

"Let me see that!" said the boy. "Crawl into this nut!" And the devil did so. When the devil had completely crawled through the wormhole, the boy plugged the hole with a twig.

"Now I've got you there!" said the boy, and put the nut in his pocket.

When the boy had walked a ways, he came to a blacksmith shop. He went in and asked the blacksmith to crack the nut for him.

"Oh, yes, that's easily done," said the smith, and he took his smallest hammer, placed the nut on the anvil and struck it–but the nut did not crack. So the smith took a bigger hammer, but neither was that heavy enough. Then the smith took an even larger hammer, but this didn't do it either. Then the blacksmith became angry. He took his very biggest sledgehammer.

"I'll get you cracked yet!" said the smith, and he struck the nut with his biggest sledgehammer using all his strength. The nut was smashed to smithereens, half the roof of the smithy flew off, and the walls crackled as if the smithy was tumbling down.

"I believe the devil himself was in that nut!" said the blacksmith.

And the boy said, "Yes, he was!"

Stupid Men And Shrewish Wives

From <u>Folktales of Norway</u> edited by R. Th. Christiansen and translated by Pat Shaw Iversen, p. 206. Collected by P. Chr. Asbjørnsen in Sogn in 1847. Based on a story in the Icelandic Legends. Variants of this tale are found throughout Europe and in the Near East as well..

There were once two wives who were always quarreling, the way some wives do now and then, and, as they had nothing better to quarrel about, they started bickering about their husbands: about which one was the more stupid of the two. The longer they quarreled, the angrier they grew, and at last they were on the verge of coming to blows. For one thing is certain, as the old saying goes: "A quarrel is more easily stirred than stilled, and it's a bad thing when common sense is lacking."

The first wife said that there was not a thing she could not make her husband believe if she but said that it was true, for he was as gullible as the *trolls*! The second wife said that no matter how wrong it might be, she could make her husband do anything if she said it should be done, for he was the kind who could not see through a ladder.

"Well, let's see which one of us can fool them the best. Then we'll find out which husband is the stupidest," they said, and this they agreed to do.

Now, when her husband came home from the woods, the first wife cried, "Heaven help me! Why, this is awful! You must be sick—if you are not already dying!"

"There's nothing wrong with me that food and drink won't cure!" said the man.

"God save me if it isn't true!" sobbed the wife. "You are getting worse and worse! You look as pale as a corpse. You had better lie down! Oh, you won't last long at all!"

Thus she carried on until she got the man to believe that he was at death's door. She got him to lie down, fold his hands, and close his eyes. Then she stretched him out, put him in a shroud, and laid him in a coffin. But, so he would not suffocate while he was in there, she made some holes in the boards so he could breathe and peek out.

The other wife? Well, she took a pair of carders, sat down, and started carding. But she had no wool on them. Her husband came in and looked at what she was doing.

"It helps little to spin without a wheel, but to card without wool, a wife is a fool," said the husband.

"Without wool?" said the wife. "Why, of course I have wool, but you can't see it because it is the finest kind!"

When the wife had finished carding, she got out the spinning wheel and started to spin.

"Nay! This is going right to the dogs!" said the husband. "Why, you're sitting there whirling and wearing out your wheel without anything on it!"

"Without anything on it?" said the wife. "The thread is so fine that it takes better eyes than yours to see it."

When the wife had finished spinning, she set up the loom and threaded it and wove the cloth. Then she took it off the loom, and cut it out, and sewed clothes out of it for her husband. And when the clothes were finished she hung them up in the *stabbur* loft. The man could see neither cloth nor clothes, but now he had come to believe that they were so fine that he could not see them, and so he said, "Well, as long as they're so fine, it's lucky I am to have them."

But one day his wife said to him, "Today you must go to a burial feast. The man at the North farm is getting buried today, so you have to have on your new clothes." Well, well, go to the burial feast he should, and the wife helped him on with the clothes, for they were so fine that he would tear them to pieces if he did it himself.

The other wife hired six pallbearers, and she asked the first couple to follow her dear husband to his grave. She also had a window made in one side of the coffin so that her husband might see all that went on around him.

When the hour came for removing the coffin, the other couple came as they had promised–the man stark naked–thinking everyone would admire his fine-spun, wonderfully weightless clothes. Although the coffin bearers were naturally in a sad mood, everyone could hardly help laughing when they saw the naked fool. And when the man in the coffin caught sight of him, he cried as loudly as he could, "Now I should laugh, if I were not dead!"

There was, of course, a great to-do: the burial was put off, the man was let out of the coffin, and when the story of how the wives had tricked their husbands came out, they got a public whipping at a parish court.

The Old Woman And The Fish

There was once an old woman who lived in a poor little place in the woods. Her husband had died long ago, and her children worked for people here and there in the parish. It was lonesome and hard with heavy work to be done there alone in her little hut. A comfortable and pleasant life she had never had, but when one has to live, one doesn't die easily or quickly, so one must take the world as it is and be satisfied. There was nothing else to do.

So she was thinking one day as she was pulling a pail of water from the well. She had this steep hill she had to climb with her water pail.

And then, she thought, before she could heat the water for her coffee, she had to split some kindling for her fire, and her axe was so rusty and dull that chopping with it was almost impossible! And all this would take so long she would be too tired to work at her loom, and the cloth she was weaving would never be so long she could make something with it! So many things were wrong, she had so many things to complain about–and complain she did! Much and often!

Now it so happened that when she finally pulled up her pail of water, in the pail was a fish! This she didn't object to!

"A fish doesn't often come into my pot!" she said to herself, and thought now she would have a really festive meal!

But this was no stupid fish she had caught this time. This one could talk!

"Let me go!" said the fish.

The woman stared. A fish that could talk! Never in the world had she seen such a fish! "Are you so much better than all other fish that you are too good to be eaten?" she asked.

"It's a wise person who doesn't eat everything that he lays his hands on. Just let me go, and you shall see you won't be unrewarded," said the fish.

"A fish in a pail suits me better than all those swimming around in the stream," said the woman, "and what you can hold in your hand, you can also get into the pan."

"That could be so," said the fish, "but if you will do as I say, you shall have three wishes!"

"Wish with one hand and wave with the other! A promise is a good thing, but keeping a promise is better. I don't believe much in your promise until I get you in the pan," said the woman.

"Watch your tongue and mark my words! Make three wishes, then you will see how things go!" said the fish.

The old woman knew what she wanted to wish, and there couldn't be much wrong with finding out if the fish **could** grant her wishes.

She thought about that steep hill and carrying her pails of water up it. "I wish the buckets would go by themselves to the well and carry water up the hill," said the old woman.

"That they shall do," said the fish.

Then the old woman thought of her axe how old and dull it was. "I wish that what I hit shall break!" she said.

"So shall it be!" said the fish.

Then the old woman thought of her weaving on the loom—and how slowly the cloth grew in length. "I wish that what I pull shall grow long!" she wished.

"So it shall be!" said the fish. "Now drop me into the well again!"

That she did.

And that very instant the buckets, filled with water, began to plod and bump their way up the steep hill.

"Have you ever seen the like!" exclaimed the old woman. She was so pleased she sat down on the well cover and slapped her knees in delight.

"Crack! Crack!" she heard, and both legs broke off at the knees. There she was left sitting on the well cover!

Now there was **really** trouble! The old woman cried and carried on. Her eyes ran and her nose ran—because the nose always runs when one cries really hard. So she had to blow her nose, and she blew it and wiped it on her apron, and the more she wiped it, the longer her nose grew!

And this is what she got for her wishes! And there she sat! And there she probably still sits, on the well cover.

The Boy Who Went To The North Wind

A combination of magic and non-magic. The boy gets "his rights" in a swift ending.

There was once an old woman who had a son, and since she was old and feeble her son was going to the *stabbur* to get meal for the noonday porridge. But when he stepped out on the *stabbur* threshold, the North Wind came, took the meal and blew it up into the air. The boy went back into the *stabbur* and got more meal, but when he stepped through the door, the North Wind again came and blew the meal away. The same thing happened the third time. Then the boy became angry. He thought it was unreasonable that the North Wind would do this, so he thought he would go find the North Wind and demand his meal.

The boy started off. The way was long. He walked and he walked. Finally he reached the North Wind.

"Good day," said the boy, "and *takk for sidst*."

"Good day," said the North Wind in his coarse deep voice, "and *takk for sidst*. And what do you want?"

"Oh," said the boy, "I want to ask you if you will be so good as to give me back the meal you took from me on the *stabbur* steps. We have so little as it is, and if you are going to keep the meal, it will be starve-to-death for us."

"I don't have any meal," said the North Wind, "but since you are in need, here is a tablecloth which will provide all you wish when you merely say, 'Cloth–spread, and provide all kinds of delicious food!'"

The boy was well pleased with this gift.

The way home was too long to reach in one day, so the boy stopped at an inn for the night. When all the guests at the inn were gathered for the evening meal, the boy went to a corner table, put down his tablecloth and said, "Cloth–spread, and provide all kinds of delicious food!" Before the boy finished speaking, the cloth did as asked. All the guests thought this was a wonderful thing, but no one liked it better than the innkeeper's wife. How **easy** everything would be if she had this cloth! No cooking or baking, no table setting, and no serving at such a table, she thought! So later that night, when everyone was asleep, the innkeeper's wife took the boy's tablecloth and replaced it with another just like it–but that tablecloth couldn't even serve flatbread.

Day came. The boy got up, took his tablecloth, and went home to his mother.

"Now," he said, "I have seen the North Wind. He is a fine fellow! In return for the meal he gave me this tablecloth. If I say, 'Cloth–spread, and provide all kinds of delicious food!' then I will get all the food we could need or want!"

"Of course!" said his mother, "but I won't believe that until I see it!"

The boy hurried and found a table, put the cloth on it and said, "Cloth–spread, and provide all kinds of delicious food!" But the cloth did not spread and did not provide food—not even a bit of flatbread!

"Well! There's nothing else to do but go back to the North Wind," said the boy, and off he went.

Late in the afternoon he reached the North Wind.

"Good evening," said the boy.

"Good evening," said the North Wind.

"I **must** get repaid for the meal you took from me!" said the boy. "The tablecloth you gave me wasn't good for much."

"I don't have any meal," said the North Wind, "but I have a goat that makes gold coins when you say, 'My goat–make money!'"

This the boy thought would be great. He took the goat, thanked the North Wind, and

started off for home. But since it was so late and he was so far from home, the boy again decided to stay at the inn for the night. Before he asked for either food or lodging, the boy tried the goat to see if the North Wind was right—and he was! But

the innkeeper had watched, and now he wanted the boy's goat. As soon as the boy was asleep, the innkeeper brought another goat to put in its place and took the boy's goat.

The next morning the boy started out for home. When he reached home he told his mother, "That North Wind is a kind man. This time he gave me a goat that makes gold coins if I just say, 'My goat—make money!'"

"Of **course**!" said his mother, "but this is only talk. I'll believe it when I see it!"

"My goat—make money!" said the boy. But the goat did not make money!

The boy went again to the North Wind and said the goat did **not** make gold money—and he **did** want payment for the meal blown away.

"Well, now I have nothing else to give you except the cane you see in the corner. But if you say, 'My cane—beat him!' it will continue beating someone until you say, 'My cane—stay still!'"

Since the way was long, the boy again stopped at the same inn. He now realized what had happened to both cloth and goat. The boy went to bed early and pretended to sleep. The innkeeper, who was sure the cane was special, too, found another identical cane to replace it. The same instant the innkeeper was about to make the switch, the boy said, "My cane—beat him!" and the cane began.

The innkeeper tried to escape by jumping over chairs and tables, and he begged the boy

to stop the cane. "Let the cane stop, or it will kill me!" cried the innkeeper. "You shall get your tablecloth and your goat if you only stop the beating!"

When the boy thought the innkeeper had been beaten enough, he said, "My cane–stay still!"

The boy put the tablecloth in his pocket, the cane in his hand, tied a string around the goat's horns, and went home with it all. It was fair exchange for the meal!

Per, Paul, And Espen *Askeladd*

There was once a man who had three sons, Per, Paul, and Espen *Askeladd*. Other than the three sons the man had nothing else, because he was so poor that he hadn't a needle for mending his clothes, and therefore he had often and repeatedly told them that they must go out into the world to try to earn a living, for at home with him would be nothing but starve-to-death!

Some distance away from the man's home was the King's *Gard*, and just outside the king's window there grew an oak so tall and broad that it completely shaded the palace and kept all sunlight out. The king promised much money to the one who would chop down the oak–but no one could, for as soon as one chip was cut, two grew in its place! The king also wished to have a well dug near his house–a well that would give water the year around. All his neighbors had such good wells that it seemed a shame that he, a king, didn't have one. The king promised money–and more!–but no one could do it because the *gard* was high on a hill, and as soon as one dug down a few inches, one struck solid rock.

But now the king decided he must have this work done. He had announcements made from all the churches far and wide that he would give the princess and half his kingdom to the one who could cut down the oak and dig a well which would give water the year around!

There were many who wished to try you can imagine! But no matter how hard they chopped and how hard they dug, the oak grew bigger and the ground grew no softer.

After a time the three brothers also wanted to try, and their father was pleased because, even if they didn't win the princess and half the kingdom, they might find work with some farmer who needed help. Better luck than that he couldn't wish for! So when the brothers said they wanted to try their luck at the King's *Gard*, their father immediately said yes, and so Per, Paul, and Espen *Askeladd* went on their way.

They soon came to a neighbor whose home was near a steep hill. They could hear a chopping sound some distance away.

"I wonder what is being chopped up there," said Espen *Askeladd*.

"Oh—you are always wondering!" said Per. "It is probably a woodcutter chopping firewood."

"Yes, but I think it would be fun to see anyway," said Espen, and although his brothers laughed and made fun of him, he paid no attention but went on his way up the hill following the sound, until he reached an axe chopping away at a pine log.

"Good day!" said Espen. "Are you standing here chopping?"

"Yes, and I've stood here and chopped for many long years waiting for you!" said the axe.

"Yes, yes—and here I am!" said Espen as he took the axe, knocked the head off the handle, and put both in his knapsack.

When he came back again to his brothers they made fun of him as before. "And what strange thing did you see up on the hill?" asked Paul.

"Oh–it was just an axe we heard," said Espen.

When they had walked some distance, they came to a cliff where they heard hoeing and scraping in thc rocky hillsidc.

"I wonder what is digging and scraping up there," said Espen.

"You are so wise and wondering!" said his brothers. "Haven't you ever heard the birds pecking and scraping at the trees and ground?"

"Yes–but I think it would be fun to see what it is anyway," said Espen, and paid no attention to his brothers but went on up to the cliff. When he reached the top he saw a sharp hoe digging and scraping.

"Good day!" said Espen. "Are you standing here, digging and scraping all alone?"

"Yes, I'm doing that," said the hoe. "Now I've stood here many long years and hoed and scraped, waiting for you!"

"Yes, yes," said Espen, "well, here I am!" He took the hoe, knocked it off the handle, and put both into his knapsack; then he went down to his brothers.

"It was surely something **very** strange you saw up on the hill!" said Per and Paul.

"Oh, nothing special. It was just a hoe we heard," said Espen.

They went on together for some distance and came to a brook. They were thirsty, so they stopped to get a drink.

"I really wonder where this water comes from," said Espen.

"And I really wonder if your brain is right," said Paul, "and if you aren't crazy yet, you will **wonder** yourself crazy! Haven't you ever seen water come from a **spring** to form a brook?"

"Yes–but I wonder where **this** water comes from anyway," said Espen, and started up the hill following the stream. No matter how his brothers called and laughed at him, he went his way.

As he went up the hill the stream became smaller and smaller. When he came farther, he saw a huge walnut. The water trickled out of it!

"Good day!" said Espen again. "Are you just lying here, all alone, the water trickling?"

"Yes, I'm doing that!" said the walnut. "Here I have been lying, the water trickling and running, for many long years waiting for you."

"Well, here I am!" said Espen, and he took some moss, plugged the hole in the walnut so the water wouldn't run out, put the walnut into his knapsack and went back to his brothers.

"I suppose you have seen where the water came from. That must have been very strange, wasn't it?" teased the brothers, Per and Paul.

"Yes, there was just a hole that it ran out of," said Espen. The other two laughed and made fun of him again, but Espen didn't care. "I thought it was fun to see it anyway," he said.

When they had gone some distance again, they finally came to the King's *Gard*. Now that everyone had heard the king's announcement–that he who could cut down the oak and dig the well would get the princess and half the kingdom–so many had come to try their luck–and failed!–that the oak was now twice as thick as it was before, because two chips grew for every one cut, as you remember. Therefore the king now had declared that anyone who tried and failed should be put out on an island and have both his ears clipped!

But the two brothers, Per and Paul, weren't frightened. They were sure they could chop down the oak! Per, the oldest, tried first. But he had the same luck as the other contestants: for every chip he cut away, two more grew. So the king's men clipped his ears, and Per was taken out to an island.

Paul still wanted to try, but when he had chopped two or three times all could **see** the oak grow. So the king's men took Paul out on the island, too, and clipped his ears even shorter than Per's, for they thought he should have learned a lesson from his brother's experience.

Now Espen wanted his turn.

"If you really want to look like a marked sheep, we'll clip your ears now, and you won't need to even try!" said the king, angry because the brothers had failed.

"I would at least like the fun of trying," said Espen, so they let him try. Espen took the axe out of his knapsack and fastened it to the axe handle.

"Chop away!" Espen said, and at once the chips flew. It didn't take long before the oak had to fall! When that was done Espen opened the knapsack, took out the hoe and fastened it to the handle.

"Dig away!" Espen said, and immediately the hoe began digging and scraping so the gravel and rocks flew! Before long the well was dug. When it had gotten as big and deep as he wished, Espen stopped the digging, took out the walnut and put it in one corner of the well. Then he removed the moss that had plugged the hole so the water could escape.

"Trickle and run!" said Espen, and after a time the well was full of water.

So Espen had chopped down the oak which had shaded the king's windows and had provided a well which would furnish water all year, so he received the princess and half the kingdom as the king had promised.

It was a good thing that Per and Paul had lost their ears, for otherwise they would have heard–time and time again–that Espen *Askeladd* had not **wondered** so very wrong!

Gudbrand On The Hillside

After the foolish exchanges, the ending is unexpected—and satisfying.

There was once upon a time a man whose name was Gudbrand. He had a farm far up on the mountainside, and so they called him Gudbrand on the Hillside.

Gudbrand and his wife lived so happily together and agreed so well that whatever the man did, the wife thought no one could have done better. No matter what Gudbrand did, his wife thought it was always the right thing.

They lived on their own farm, had a hundred dollars at the bottom of their chest, and two cows in their cowshed.

One day the woman said to Gudbrand, "I think we ought to go to town with one of the cows and sell it so we may have some ready money. We're pretty well off and ought to have some loose change in our pockets like other people. The hundred dollars in the chest we mustn't touch, but I can't see what we want with more than one cow. It will be much better for us to sell one, for then I shall have only one cow to look after instead of the two I now have to mind and feed."

Yes, Gudbrand thought that was well and sensibly spoken. He took the cow at once and went to town to sell it, but when he got there, no one would buy the cow.

"Ah, well," thought Gudbrand, "I may as well take the cow home again. I know I have

both stall and food for it, and the way home is no longer than it was here." So Gudbrand started out for home with the cow.

When Gudbrand got a bit on the way, he met a man who had a horse to sell. Gudbrand thought it was better to have a horse than a cow, and so he exchanged the cow for a horse.

Gudbrand went on a bit farther and met a man who was driving a fat pig before him. Gudbrand thought it would be better to have a fat pig than a horse, so he exchanged with the man.

Gudbrand went a bit farther, and then he met a man with a goat. As Gudbrand thought it was better to have a goat than a pig, he exchanged with the man who had the goat.

Then Gudbrand went a long way until he met a man who had a sheep. Gudbrand exchanged his goat for the sheep, for he thought it was always better to have a sheep than a goat.

When he had gone a bit farther, Gudbrand met a man with a goose, and so he exchanged the sheep for the goose. And when Gudbrand had gone a long, long way, he met a man with a cock. Gudbrand exchanged the goose with him, for he thought, "It is surely better to have a cock than a goose."

Gudbrand walked on until late in the day, when he began to feel hungry. So he sold the cock for twelve shillings and bought food for himself. "It is always better to keep body and soul together than to have a rooster," thought Gudbrand.

Gudbrand set off again for home. He came to his neighbor's place, and there he went in.

"How did you do in town?" asked the neighbor.

"Oh, only so-so," said Gudbrand. "I can't boast of my luck, nor can I grumble at it either." And then Gudbrand told them how it had gone from first to last.

"Well! You'll have a fine reception when you get home to your wife!" said the neighbor. "Heaven help you! I should not like to be in your place!"

"I think I might have fared worse," said Gudbrand, "but whether I have fared well or ill, I have such a kind wife that she never says anything no matter what I do."

"Aye, so you say, but you won't get me to believe it," said the neighbor.

"Shall we make a bet on it?" asked Gudbrand. "I have a hundred dollars in my chest at home. Will you match that?"

So they made the wager. Gudbrand stayed until evening when it began to get dark, and then they went together to Gudbrand's farm. The neighbor was to remain outside the door and listen while Gudbrand went in to his wife.

"Good evening!" said Gudbrand when he came in.

"Good evening!" said his wife. "God be praised you are back again!"

"Yes, here I am," said Gudbrand, and then the wife asked him how he had got on in town.

"Oh, so-so," answered Gudbrand. "Not much to brag of. When I came to town, no one would buy the cow, so I exchanged it for a horse."

"Oh, I'm so glad of that!" said the woman. "We are pretty well off, and we ought to drive to church like other people, and when we can afford to keep a horse, I don't see why we should not have one. Run out, children, and put the horse in the stable!"

"Well, I haven't got the horse after all," said Gudbrand, "for when I had got a bit on the way, I exchanged it for a pig."

"Dear me!" cried the woman. "That's the very thing I should have done myself! I'm so glad of that, for now we can have some bacon in the house and something to offer people when they come to see us. What do we want with a horse? People would only say we had become so grand that we could no longer walk to church. Run out, children, and let the pig in."

"But I haven't got the pig either," said Gudbrand, "for when I had got a bit farther on the road, I exchanged it for a milk goat."

"Dear, dear! How well you manage everything!" cried Gudbrand's wife. "When I really come to think of it, what do I want with the pig? People would only say, 'Over yonder people eat up everything they have.' No, now that I have a goat I can have both milk and cheese and keep the goat into the bargain. Let in the goat, children."

"But I haven't got the goat either," said Gudbrand. "When I got a bit on the way, I exchanged the goat and got a fine sheep for it."

"Well!" shouted the woman. "You do everything just as I should wish it—just as if I had been there myself! What do we want with a goat? I should have to climb up

hill and down dale to get it home at night. No, when I have a sheep I can have wool and clothes in the house and food as well. Run out, children, and let in the sheep."

"But I haven't got the sheep any longer," said Gudbrand, "for when I had got a bit on the way, I exchanged it for a goose."

"Well! Thank you for that!" said the woman. "And many thanks, too! What do I want with a sheep? I have neither wheel nor spindle, and I do not care to toil and drudge making clothes. We can buy clothes now as before. Now I can have goose fat, which I have so long been wishing for, and some feathers to stuff that little pillow of mine. Run, children, and let in the goose!"

"Well, I haven't got the goose, either," said Gudbrand. "When I got a bit farther on the way, I exchanged it for a cock."

"Well! I don't know how you can think of it all!" said the woman. "It is just as if I had done it all myself!–A cock! Why, it's just the same as if you had bought an eight-day clock, for every morning the cock will crow at four so we can be up in good time! What do we want with a goose? I can't make goose fat, and I can easily fill my pillow with some soft grass. Run, children, and let in the cock."

"But I haven't got a cock either," said Gudbrand, "for when I had got a bit farther, I became so terribly hungry I had to sell the cock for sixpence to get some food to keep body and soul together."

"Heaven be praised you did that!" cried the woman. "Whatever you do, you always do the very thing I could have wished! Besides, what did we want with the cock? We are our own masters and can lie as long as we like in the mornings. Heaven be praised as long as I have got you back again—you who manage everything so well! I shall neither want cock, nor goose, nor pig, nor cow!"

Gudbrand then opened the door. "Have I won the hundred dollars now?" he asked. And the neighbor was obliged to confess that he had.

Why The Sea Is Salt

Translated by Sir G. W. Dasent from the tales collected by Peter Christen Asbjørnsen and Jørgen Moe. Their original title–it seems–was "Kvernen Paa Havet's Bund" which translated would be "The Hand Mill in Davy Jones Locker" or "On the Bottom of the Ocean".

Once in the olden, olden days there were two brothers, one was rich and the other poor. When Christmas Eve came, the poor brother had not a crumb of bread nor a drop of ale in the house, so he went to his brother and asked him for a little something for Christmas, in God's name. Most likely it was not the first time the brother needed help–and the rich brother wasn't especially fond of him, either!

The rich brother thought a while; then he said, "If you will do what I ask, I shall give you an entire ham!"

The poor brother promised at once, and thanked him again and again.

"There you have it! Now go straight to Hell!" said the rich one, and threw the ham over to his brother.

"Well, I promised, so I had better keep my promise," said the poor brother. He took the ham and started off. He walked and he walked the entire day. Just at dusk he came to a well-lighted place. "This must be the place," thought the brother with the ham.

Outside, in the woodshed, stood an old man with a long beard, chopping Christmas wood.

"Good evening!" said the brother with the ham.

"Good evening to you! And where are you going so late in the day?" asked the old man.

"I'm going to Hell, if I've found the right way," answered the poor brother.

"Oh, yes, you've gone the right way. It is right here," said the old man. "And when you go in, everyone will want to buy your ham, because ham is seldom seen in Hell. But you must not sell it unless you get the *kvern*–the small hand mill which stands behind the door. When you come out again, I'll tell you how to use it. This *kvern* is useful for many things."

The brother with the ham thanked him for the useful information. Then he knocked at the Devil's door.

When he got in, all went just as the old man had said. All the devils, both large and small, swarmed around him like ants around an anthill, and each tried to outbid the others in order to get the ham.

"To tell the truth," said the poor brother, "my wife and I were going to have this ham for our Christmas dinner, but since you have all set your hearts on it, I suppose I must sell it to you. But if I sell it at all, I'll have for it that *kvern* behind the door yonder."

At first the Devil wouldn't hear of such a bargain and argued and haggled with him, but the brother stuck to what he said, and at last the Devil had to part with his *kvern*.

When the poor brother got out into the yard, he asked the old woodcutter how he was to handle the *kvern*. After he had learned how to use it, he thanked the old man and went off home as fast as he could, but still the clock had struck twelve on Christmas Eve before he reached his own door.

"Wherever in the world have you been?" exclaimed his old dame. "Here I have sat, hour after hour, waiting and watching, without so much as two sticks to lay together under the Christmas broth!"

"Oh," said the poor brother, "I couldn't get back before, for I had to go a long way first for one thing and then for another, but now you shall see what you shall see."

So he put the *kvern* on the table and bade it first to grind candles, then a tablecloth, then meat, then ale, and so on, until they had everything that was nice for Christmas fare. He had only to speak the word, and the *kvern* ground out what he wanted.

The old dame stood by blessing her stars, and she kept asking where he had gotten this wonderful *kvern*, but he wouldn't tell her.

"It doesn't matter where I got it from. You see the *kvern* is a good one and the millstream never freezes, that's enough."

So he ground meat and drink and much more–enough to last until Twelfth Day–and on the third day he asked all his friends and his kin to his house and gave a great feast. Now, when his rich brother saw all that was on the table and all that was in the larder, he grew quite spiteful and wild, for he could not bear that his brother should have anything.

"It was only on Christmas Eve," the rich brother said to the rest, "he was in such straits that he came and asked for a morsel of food in God's name, and now he gives a feast as if he were a count or a king!" Then he turned to his brother and said, "But where in hell did you get all this wealth?"

"From behind the door," answered the owner of the *kvern*, for he didn't care to let the cat out of the bag. But later on in the evening when he had had a drop too much, he could keep his secret no longer and brought out the *kvern* and said, "There you see what has gotten me all this wealth!" And so he made the *kvern* grind out both this and that.

When the rich brother saw it, he set his heart on having the *kvern*. After a great deal of coaxing he got it, but he had to pay three hundred dollars for it, and his brother bargained to keep it until after hay harvest. "For if I keep it until then, I can make it grind meat and drink that will last for years," he thought. So you may fancy the *kvern* did not become rusty from lack of use! And, when hay harvest came, the rich brother got the *kvern*, but the other took care not to teach him how to handle it.

It was evening when the rich brother got the *kvern* home. The next morning he told his wife to go into the hayfield and toss the hay while the mowers cut the grass, and he would stay at home and get the dinner ready. So, when dinnertime drew near, he put the *kvern* on the kitchen table and said, "Grind herring and broth, and grind them good and fast!"

So the *kvern* began to grind herring and broth until all the dishes were full, then all the tubs were full, and so on until the kitchen floor was quite covered. The rich brother twisted and turned at the *kvern* to get it to stop, but for all his twisting and fingering, the *kvern* kept on grinding, and in a little while the broth rose so high that the man was likely to drown. He threw open the kitchen door and ran into the parlor, but it wasn't long before the *kvern* had ground the parlor full, too, and it was only at the risk of his life that the man could get hold of the latch of the house door through the stream of broth. When he got the door open, he ran out and set off down the road with the stream of herring and broth at his heels, roaring like a waterfall over the whole farm.

Now his old dame, who was in the field tossing hay, thought it a long time to dinner, and at last she said, "Well, though the master doesn't call us home, we may as well go. Maybe he finds it hard work to boil the broth and needs my help."

The men were willing enough, so they sauntered homeward, but just as they had gotten a little way up the hill, what should they meet but herring and broth and bread all running and dashing and splashing together in a stream, and the master himself running before them for his life. As he passed them he bawled out, "Would to heaven each of you had a hundred throats! But take care you do not drown in the broth!"

Away he went, as though the Evil One were at his heels, to his brother's house and begged him, for God's sake, to take back the *kvern* that instant, for, said he, "If it grinds only one hour more, the whole parish will be swallowed up by herring and broth!"

But the poor brother wouldn't hear of taking the *kvern* back until the other paid him down three hundred dollars more.

So the poor brother got both the money and the *kvern*, and it wasn't long before he set up a farmhouse far nicer than the one in which his brother lived. With the *kvern* he ground so much gold that he covered his house with plates of gold. As the farm lay by the seaside, the golden house gleamed and glistened far away over the sea. All who sailed by put ashore to see the rich man in the golden house and to see the wonderful *kvern*, the fame of which spread far and wide till there was no one who hadn't heard of it.

So one day there came a skipper who wanted to see the *kvern*, and the first thing he asked was if the *kvern* could grind salt.

"Grind salt!" said the owner. "I should just think it could. It can grind anything!"

When the skipper heard that, he said he must have the *kvern*, cost what it would; for if he only had it, he thought he should be rid of his long voyages across the stormy seas for a lading of salt.

Well, at first the owner wouldn't hear of parting with the *kvern*, but the skipper begged and prayed so hard that at last the owner let him have it–but the skipper had to pay many, many thousand dollars for it. Now, when the skipper had the *kvern* on his back, he soon made off with it, for he was afraid lest the owner should change his mind. So the skipper took no time to ask how to handle the *kvern* but got on board his ship as fast as he could and set sail.

When the skipper had sailed a good way off, he brought the *kvern* on deck and said, "Grind salt, and grind both good and fast."

Well, the *kvern* began to grind salt so it poured out like water. When the skipper had the ship full of salt, he wished to stop the *kvern*, but whichever way the skipper turned it, and however much he tried, it was no good. The *kvern* kept grinding on, and the heap of salt grew higher and higher, and at last down sank the ship.

There lies the *kvern* at the bottom of the sea and grinds away this very day, and that's why the sea is salt.

The Princess Who Couldn't Be Silenced

There was once a king whose daughter was so clever with words that no one could silence her. Finally the king sent word to the highways and byways that whoever could silence her should be given the princess and half the kingdom. You can believe many were interested in this challenge, for such a prize–a princess and half the kingdom!–is not given each day!

The gate to the King's *Gard* was never still: they came from east and from west, riding or walking, alone or in groups–but no one could silence the princess.

Finally the king gave notice: Anyone who tried to silence the princess and did not succeed should be branded on both ears with his large branding iron. It was right there on the *gard* and might as well be useful.

There were three brothers who had heard about the princess. Since they had very little at home, they wanted to go out in the world and try their luck. They might as well see if one of them could win the princess and half the kingdom. The three brothers were good friends and got along well, so they started off together. The youngest was named *Askeladden*.

When they had gone a short distance *Askeladden* found a dead bird. "I found! I found!" he called out.

"What did you find?" asked the brothers.

"I found a dead bird!" said *Askeladden*.

"*Fy*! Throw it away! Why would you keep **that**?" asked the brothers who thought that they were much wiser than *Askeladden*.

"Oh, I have things to do and things to keep. I think I'll keep it," said *Askeladden*.

They walked farther on and *Askeladden* found a long, soft willow root. "I found! I found!" he shouted.

"What did you find now?" asked the brothers.

"I found a long willow root!" *Askeladden* answered.

"How could you use that? Throw it away!" said the brothers.

"Oh, I have things to do and things to keep. I think I'll keep it," said *Askeladden*.

When they had gone a bit farther *Askeladden* found a broken piece of pottery. "I found! I found!" he shouted.

"Now what did you find?" the brothers asked.

"Part of a broken pot!" *Askeladden* answered.

"That is nothing to bother carrying around–just throw it away!" they said.

"Oh, I have things to do and things to keep. I think I will keep it," said *Askeladden*.

They walked on. Then *Askeladden* found an old crooked ram's horn, and very nearby he found another just like it! "Boys! I found! I found!" he called.

"What did you find now?" asked the brothers.

"Two ram's horns!" answered *Askeladden*.

"*Isj*! Throw them! What **could** you use those for?" they asked.

"No–I have things to do and things to keep, so I think I will keep them!" said *Askeladden*.

In a little while *Askeladden* again found something: a wedge. "*Nei*, boys! I found! I found!" he called.

"You are really great at finding things!" said the oldest brother. "What did you find now?"

"I found a wedge!" *Askeladden* answered.

"Throw it away! What could you do with that?" said the other brother.

"No–I have things to do and things to keep, so I think I'll keep it," said *Askeladden*.

Now they were crossing the fields near the King's *Gard*. *Askeladden* bent down and picked up something. It was an old, well-worn shoe sole. "Boys! I found! I found!" he said.

"If only you found some **sense** before we get there! **So**–what did you find this time?" asked the brothers.

"An old worn shoe sole!" said *Askeladden*.

"*Isj da*! **That** was something to pick up! Throw it! Whatever would you do with something like that?" the brothers exclaimed.

"No–I have things to do and things to keep, so I had better keep this if I'm going to win the princess and half the kingdom!" said *Askeladden*.

"Yes–it looks as if you will do that!" mocked the brothers.

Finally they were there–and there was the king's daughter!

The oldest brother went first. "Good day!" he said.

"Good day again," the princess answered and squirmed.

"It's very warm here!" said the brother.

"It's warmer in the firepot," said the princess, for there lay the branding iron, ready and waiting.

When the oldest brother saw that, everything went wrong at once, and he was finished!

And it went no better for the next brother. "Good day!" he said.

"Good day again," the princess said and squirmed.

"It's **very** hot in here!" said the brother.

"It's hotter in the firepot," the princess said, and with that the brother lost his words, his voice, and his courage–and the branding iron did its work.

Now came *Askeladden*. "Good day!" he said.

"Good day again," the princess answered, and she squirmed and wiggled.

"It's good and warm here," said *Askeladden*.

"It's warmer in the firepot," the princess answered, no friendlier the third time than with the first two brothers.

"Then may I roast my bird there?" asked *Askeladden*.

"I am afraid she will burst," said the king's daughter.

"No problem," said *Askeladden*, "I can tie this willow root around it."

"Oh–it's too loose!" said the princess.

"I'll drive in a wedge," said *Askeladden*, and he took out the wedge.

"The fat could drip off the bird!" said the king's daughter.

"I can hold this underneath to catch the drips!" said *Askeladden*, and he took up the broken pot.

"Your words are so crooked they twist everything I say!" said the king's daughter.

"No, my words are not crooked and twisted–but this is!" said *Askeladden*, holding up a ram's horn.

"Well! Have you ever seen the like!" the princess exclaimed.

"Yes–here is the like!" said *Askeladden*, taking out the second ram's horn.

"You are here to wear me out so I'll stop talking, aren't you?" said the princess.

"No, you aren't worn out–but **this** is worn out," *Askeladden* said, taking out the worn shoe sole.

And now the princess **was** speechless.

"And now you are mine!" said *Askeladden*, and he got the half kingdom as well!

Nail Soup

A common folktale to show how man uses his wits to survive. The French version is "Stone Soup."

There was once a tramp who was wandering in the woods up north. Houses were few and far between. It was getting late in the day, and the tramp needed shelter for the night. He looked around, saw no house but thought he smelled smoke.

"Aha!" thought the tramp, "Where there is smoke, there is fire; where there is fire, there is warmth; and—who knows—there might be food and shelter, too!" So the tramp followed his nose, which led him to a house. A woman was outside the door.

"Good evening, and well met!" said the tramp.

"Good evening to you!" said the woman, "and where are you going?"

"South of the Sun and East of the Moon," said the tramp. "And now I am on my way there, for now I have seen the entire world, except for this parish."

"You have traveled much," said the woman, "and what might be your errand here?"

He would very much like shelter for the night, the tramp said.

"I might have known!" said the woman. Well, her husband was not home, and they didn't take in lodgers, she told the tramp.

"Oh, please, kind lady, don't be difficult," the tramp said. "After all, we are both human beings, and the Good Book says we should help others."

"Help! Help!" exclaimed the woman. "Who helps me? Even when I haven't a crumb in the house!" No–he would just have to find shelter some other place.

But the tramp wasn't one to give up at the first rebuff. He was like a dog with a bone–he gnawed away until the woman finally gave in and agreed he could sleep on the floor that night.

That was a good offer, the tramp said, and for that she should have thanks. "Better on the floor awake than in the woods freezing."

Now the tramp became very polite and asked very nicely if he could get some food.

"Where should I get food?" the woman said. "I've gone all day without even a crust of bread!"

But this tramp was clever. "Oh, poor grandmother! You must be **very** hungry!" he said. "I will have to be the one to invite you to a feast!"

"You invite me to a feast?" the woman asked. The tramp didn't look able to invite anyone to a feast.

He who has traveled far has learned to keep his wits about him, so the tramp at once said, "Lend me a kettle, Grandmother."

Now the woman became curious. She found a kettle. The tramp poured water in the kettle and placed it over the fire and added wood until the flames came up around the pot. Next he took a five-inch nail from his pocket, turned it three times in his hand, and then put it into the kettle.

The woman's eyes grew big! "What is this going to be?" she asked.

"Nail Soup," said the tramp, and he began to stir.

"Nail Soup?" asked the woman.

"Yes–Nail Soup," said the tramp, stirring away.

Much had the woman seen, and much had she done, but **never** had she even **heard** about making soup on a nail! That was something poor people needed to do–and she must learn how.

"Then watch!" said the tramp and stirred the kettle. "This usually is very good soup," he said, "but this time it may seem quite thin, for I

have used this same nail all week! If I only had a handful or two of meal, it would help. But what one doesn't have, one shouldn't wish for!" and he stirred away.

"Why," said the woman, "there might be some meal left in the bag!" and she brought it.

The tramp added and stirred—and admired his soup. "Now if we only had a meat bone and maybe some small potatoes, we'd have a feast fit for a king!" he said as he stirred and stirred.

Now the woman remembered she **had** some small potatoes, and she found a meat bone, too! Whatever she found, the tramp added to the soup, and he stirred and stirred, and she stared and stared.

"This would be just the kind of soup the king would have for supper if we only had some carrots and an onion," the tramp said, "but what we don't have, we don't wish for!" But the woman found both carrots and onion, and the tramp added those and stirred and stirred.

The woman by now had crouched down, elbows on knees, staring first at the stirred soup and then at the tramp.

Finally the tramp took up the nail. "Now the soup is ready, so now we are feasting like a king and queen! But if the king and queen were eating, they would have a tablecloth on the table and at least have bread and butter with it!" he said.

128

By now the woman felt like a queen, too, so she found a tablecloth, set the table, found bread and butter and other things, too. Never had she had such a meal! Never had she tasted such soup! And that cooked just on a nail!

That night the tramp slept in the bed, and the woman on the floor–and the next morning she awakened him with a cup of steaming coffee!

When the tramp left the next day, the woman gave him a shiny silver dollar for teaching her how to make soup on a nail! "Thanks, thanks, and many thanks!" the woman said. "Now I can have good meals any time, now that I have learned to make soup on a nail!"

As he left, the tramp said, "It's not hard when you have good things to add to it!"

But the woman watched him leave and said to herself, "Such folks don't grow on every bush!"

The Man Who Would Keep House

There was once a man who was so cross and disagreeable he never thought his wife did enough work in the house. He came home one evening during haying and crabbed and swore and complained until the air around him was blue!

"Oh, dear! Don't be so ill-tempered, father," said his wife. "Tomorrow let's trade work. I'll go out in the hay field to help the men, and you can stay home and keep house."

Now that was a good idea, thought the man, so this he surely would agree to do.

Early the next morning the wife took the scythe and went out into the meadow with the other workers ready to start cutting the grass.

The man was ready to start the housework. First of all, he wanted to churn butter. When he had churned a while, he became thirsty and went into the cellar to tap some ale. While he was filling the ale bowl, he heard the pig had gotten into the kitchen. The man rushed up with the tap in his hand, up the cellar steps as fast as he could go, to prevent the pig from upsetting the churn–but the pig had already tipped the churn and was busy slurping up the cream which had run out over the kitchen floor. The man became so angry he forgot the ale–and the tap–and chased the pig. He caught up with it in the doorway and gave it such a powerful kick that it lay there motionless. Now the man remembered the ale and the tap in his hand! But when he got down into the cellar, all the ale had run out, and all that was left was an empty keg.

The man then went out to the cooler and found cream to fill his churn, and again he started churning–for butter he must have for the noon meal. When he had churned a while, he suddenly remembered the cow! It was still in the cow barn and yet had been given no water or hay, and the sun was high in the sky! It was too late–and too far–to take her out to pasture. But he knew much grass grew on the thatched roof. That's where she could graze! The house lay next to a steep hill, and if he put down a plank from the hill to the roof, he was sure he could get the cow up there. But the churn? He couldn't leave it, because the child was crawling around and might tip it, so he put the churn on his back. But first he must give the cow water before he put her up on the roof. The man took a bucket to the well, but as he bent over to lower the bucket, the cream ran out of the churn down his neck and into the well.

It was now soon noon, and the man still hadn't made butter! He had better just make porridge for the noon meal. He put water in a kettle and hung it over the fire. Then he remembered the cow on the

roof. She could fall off the roof and break a leg! So he went up on the roof with a rope. He tied one end of the rope to the cow's neck, dropped the rope down the chimney, went in and tied the other end of the rope around his thigh.

Now the water was boiling, and the porridge needed stirring. While he was stirring the porridge, the cow fell off the roof anyway and pulled the man up the chimney. There he was–stuck!–and there the cow hung outside the wall, swinging between heaven and earth and could go neither up nor down.

The housewife had waited for the call to come home for dinner. No call came, so she finally started home. There she saw the cow swinging and swaying in the wind. She cut the rope with her scythe. At the same moment the man fell down through the chimney, and when the woman came in, there he stood on his head in the porridge pot!

The Woman Against The Stream

As noted, many legends and many tales have a great many variants. This is one of the many variants of this tale.

There was once a man who had a wife, and she was so contrary and mean that it was not easy to get along with her. The man—well he tried his best, but with poor results, for whatever he wanted, his wife wanted the direct opposite. So it was one Sunday morning in late summer when they were out walking in the fields to see how the crops were faring.

When they came to the field across the river the man said, "Yes, that grain is ripe. Tomorrow it must be cut!"

"Yes, tomorrow we can clip this field," said his wife.

"What do you mean, 'clip the field?' Aren't we going to use the scythe and cut it?" asked the man.

No—clip the field is what they would do, meant the wife.

"There is nothing worse than little sense," said the man, "but you must have lost the little you had! Have you ever seen anyone clip a field?" he asked.

"I don't know much, and I don't want to know much," said the woman, "but this I

know: this field shall be clipped and not cut. No more talk is needed," she said. "It shall be clipped."

So they walked on and argued and quarreled until they came to the bridge over the stream where the water was deep.

"There is an old saying," said the man, "that good tools make good work. I believe the work would be anything but good if we clip the field with the sheep shears! Can't we rather use the scythe to cut the grain?" he asked.

"No! No! Clip! Clip! Clip!" shouted the woman, and she jumped up and down and clipped the air with her fingers–almost at the poor man's nose! And then, in her anger, she stumbled and fell into the stream!

"Old habits are hard to break," thought the man, "but it would be amusing if I could **just this once** be right!" So he lay down on the bridge, reached into the water, and got hold of his wife's hair so he could hold her head above the water.

"Shall we cut the field?" he asked.

"No! Clip! Clip! Clip!" screamed the woman.

"Yes, I'll teach you to clip, that I will!" thought the man, and he ducked her under the water, but it didn't help. They should **clip** she said when he pulled her up again.

"I can't believe but that the woman is crazy!" said the man to himself. "Many are crazy and don't know it, and some have good sense and don't show it. But I must try once more!"

The man had no sooner ducked the woman's head down again before her hand came out of the water and her fingers began clipping like scissors!

Now the man became really angry and ducked her head down, both well and long. But suddenly the hand fell down, the fingers stopped clipping, and the woman became very heavy.

"Do you want to pull me in with you?" said the man–as he lost his grasp. And the woman was left there.

But after a time the man thought it seemed sad that she shouldn't be buried in Christian soil, so he searched down the river, but found nothing. Other people from the area looked and looked, but for all their searching, they didn't find the woman.

"No," said the man, "this was a woman who, when she lived, was contrary. She would still be contrary—she could not be otherwise now. We must search upstream, beyond the rapids. Perhaps she has floated herself up there."

So the searchers went above the rapids—and there she lay. This was right, for she was the woman against the stream.

GLOSSARY

The glossary contains names, terms, and clarifications. Keep in mind that Norse is a phonetic language. The result is that each spells the word as it sounds in **his own dialect**. The regional differences serve to enrich the end result.

Askelad	"Ash Boy;" the younger brother; the "hero."
Askeladden	"The ash boy."
Berg-folk	"People of the hills;" *huldre*-folk; underworld "people."
Carders	Used to untangle wool.
Changeling	A *huldre*-child exchanged for a human child; sometimes used to explain the birth of an abnormal or deformed baby.
Dovre Mountain	A mountain in Norway; home of the underworld "people."
Draug	Supernatural beings on land or usually in the sea; the "living dead" in some dialects.
Fjord	An inlet of the sea.
Fossegrim	"Creatures" of waterfalls. (See *nøkken*.)

Fy	Ugh! Whew!
Gangferd	The unhappy ghosts of the dead who may compel the living to follow. (See *oskerei*.)
Gard	Norwegian house and/or farm.
Gardvord	The spirit and guardian of the house or farm; also called *tomte gubben* or *tunkall*.
Gyger	A female *troll*; a giantess.
Haug-folk	"Dwellers in mounds;" the hidden or unseen beings; underworld "people," such as *huldre*-folk, *berg*-folk, *underjordiske,* etc.
Hellig Olav	St. Olav, the "perpetual King." Ruled 1015-1030. *(rex perpetuus Norwegiae)*
Himmerike	Heaven; paradise.
Hulder	A beautiful *huldre* maiden, but has a cow's tail; daughter of a *troll*.
Huldre-folk	Inclusive name for the "hidden people;" "invisible people;" sometimes referred to as *vetter* or *trolls*. (Sometimes believed to be similar to human beings.)

Huldrin   To be bewitched by a *hulder*.

Isj   Phooey! Ugh! Expressing distaste.
Isj da

Jotun   The giants; enemies of the Norse pagan gods; related to
the *trolls*

Kvern   A hand mill used for grinding grain or coffee..

Landsmaal   The language or dialect of the common man; today called *nynorsk*.

Lur   A wind instrument; a long horn used especially at the *seter*
to call cattle.

Nei   No.

Nisse   A small gnome-like spirit who is the household guardian; often a
trickster or mischief-maker.

Nøkken   Spirit of waterfalls and rivers.

Odel   Property owned under an alodial system.

Odelsbonde   Freeholder; farmer owning property under *odelsrett*.

Odelsrett	Form of property ownership acquired by a family to a farm held for at least 20 years, whereby members of the family have the right to redeem it within five years of sale.
Old Erik	A common Scandinavian name for the devil.
Oskorei	The "terrible host;" a group of spirits, which ride wildly through on Christmas Eve.
Seter	Chalet and summer dairy, usually in the mountain pasture. The unmarried women generally stayed in the chalet or cabin at the *seter* during the summer, took care of the cattle, and made butter and cheese.
Smør	Butter.
Smør øye	Butter "dot" or "eye" in porridge.
Stabbur	A storehouse for food and household equipment, usually built up on rocks or pillars to discourage animals.
Takk	Thanks.
Takk for sidst	Norse greeting to an acquaintance; "Thank you for the last time (we met)."

Ting	A community meeting to make decisions. *Storting* is Norway's Parliament.
Troll	Superhuman ogre; may vary in size and strength, but is always fearful. (Humans can outwit the *troll* because it **is** stupid.)
Tunkall	The "guardian of the house," thought to be the spirit of the original owner of a farm/house; very big.
Tusen takk	"A thousand thanks."
Tusse **Tusse-folk** **Tufte-folk**	A *troll*; the terms vary in different parts of Norway, but all are supernatural creatures; various terms used to denote *huldre*-folk.
Underjordiske	"Those under the ground;" an all-inclusive term used for *tusse*-folk, *haug*-folk, and *huldre*-folk (also called *vetter*). The *underjordiske* live on the fringe of the areas inhabited by human beings.
Vetter	An all-inclusive term for the supernatural beings living on the fringe of the area inhabited by human beings.

SELECTED READINGS

This is a list of sources consulted in writing this book. Not listed are notes from lectures in the classes at Blindern in Oslo, and my memories of the many stories read and heard from childhood and on.

Konge Sagaer (The Prose Edda)
> Snorri Sturluson
>> Translated by Dr. Gustav Storm
>> Kristiania, 1902

Norske Folke og Huldre Eventyr
> Pr. Christian Asbjørnsen and Jørgen Moe, 1852-1870
>> Translated by Trygve Knudson, 1964

Norge og Nordens Historie
> Jens Raabe
> Kristiania, 1906

Norge Gjennem Tiderne IV
> Nordahl Rolfsen
> Kristiania, 1914

Deklamationsboken
    O. E. Rølvaag
    Minneapolis, 1918

Norsk Lesebok   Bind III
        Norge i Saga og Diktning
            O. E. Rølvaag and P. J. Eikeland
            Minneapolis, 1925

Anthology of Children's Literature
    Johnson, Sickels, Sayers
    Boston, 1959

Folktales of Norway
    Ed. By Reidar Th. Christiansen
        Translated by Pat Shaw Iverson
        © 1964 by the University of Chicago. All rights reserved
            Published 1964. Second Impression 1968
            Printed in the United States of America